The Financial Role of
Multinational Enterprises

The Financial Role of Multinational Enterprises

W. A. P. MANSER

A HALSTED PRESS BOOK

JOHN WILEY & SONS
New York

Published by
Associated Business Programmes Ltd
17 Buckingham Gate SW1

Distributed by
Cassell and Co. Ltd.
35 Red Lion Square London WC1R 4SJ

First published 1973

© International Chamber of Commerce and W. A. P. Manser, 1973

This book has been printed in Great Britain
by The Anchor Press Ltd. and bound by
Wm. Brendon & Son Ltd., both of Tiptree, Essex

ISBN 0 470–56766 –X

LC 72–12259

Published in the U.S.A. by
Halsted Press, a Division
of John Wiley & Sons, Inc.,
New York

Contents

PART II – FINANCIAL MANAGEMENT

Contents   5

<h2 style="text-align:center">STATISTICAL APPENDIX</h2>

Foreword

The International Chamber of Commerce has been drawing attention for many years to the increasing importance for economic growth of international private investment, and in particular the internationalisation of production. It has sought to draw attention to the positive role that foreign investment plays in the economics of both industrialised and developing countries. It has also systematically analysed the conditions that are necessary if international investment is to be beneficial both to the investing country and to the country that receives the investment.

The multinational enterprise, even though it cannot easily or usefully be defined, can be identified essentially as the company or group of companies that operates internationally and contributes substantially to the flow of direct investment between countries.

Knowledge about the operations of multinational enterprises, their policies and their interaction with national economies, is fragmentary. The result is that no secure base exists for the formulation of sound opinions for the development of constructive policies by governments and by enterprises themselves.

In these circumstances, the International Chamber of Commerce has tried to encourage objective research leading to a greater availability of the facts upon which sound decisions can be based. It thus arranged for an independent economic study of the international corporation by Dr. Sidney E. Rolfe whose published report provided important and original information as a basis for discussion at the ICC's 1969 congress in Istanbul. That congress recommended further action by the ICC in connection with the multinational enterprise and some of the results are now available.

Thus, the ICC special committee on the international corporation, under the Chairmanship of Mr. Wilfrid Baumgartner (France), prepared a report on international corporations and the transfer of technology which was made available in April 1972 to the United Nations conference on Trade and Development in Santiago. In December 1972, the ICC published guidelines for international private investment containing detailed recommendations to investors, to the governments of the host country and to the governments of capital exporting countries drawn up by its commission on international investments and economic development whose Chairman is Dr. Pieter Kuin (Netherlands).

The financial role of the multinational enterprise is of key importance in the context of the ICC's efforts to encourage well informed discussion of the inevitable problems associated with the international flow of investment. For this reason a thorough and objective assessment seemed necessary. The ICC can congratulate itself for having persuaded Mr. W. A. P. Manser, Economic Adviser to Baring Brothers & Co. Ltd., to undertake to prepare a book on the subject which, as readers will find, provides many facts and figures not previously published, thus quantifying in a way that was not previously possible the effects of multinational business operations on capital flows and on national economies. I am confident that this will provide a lasting and valuable contribution to informed discussion of these important issues. Mr. Manser's work will, I feel sure, enable future students of this subject to see the matter in a much more accurate and factual perspective than has hitherto been the case.

WALTER HILL
Secretary General,
International Chamber of Commerce

Acknowledgements

I record my sincere thanks to the International Chamber of Commerce and its National Committees for their continued and varied practical assistance, particularly as regards putting me in touch with informed quarters; to Baring Brothers & Co., Limited, for assenting without demur to the devotion to this study of so much of my time; to the finance directors and financial staffs, too numerous to mention individually, of some 35 international companies, for their invaluable advice and factual information, including the provision, in many cases, of company financial data; to staff members of the Bank of England, the Banque de France, the Bundesbank, and the Banca d'Italia, for their kind guidance; to the UK Department of Trade & Industry, the US Department of the Treasury, and the US Department of Commerce, for much factual data and some invaluable special analyses; to the International Monetary Fund, the Organisation for Economic Co-operation & Development, the Development Assistance Directorate, the European Economic Commission, and the Economic Commission for Europe, for their kind advice, and in some cases, substantial additional information; to the Deutsche Bank, the Bank of London & South America, the Banque de Bruxelles, and the Fédération Bancaire de la Communauté, for their information and comment; to the Confederation of British Industry, the Conseil National du Patronat Français, BIAC, and UNICE, for their practical help; and to Mr. C. T. Taylor, of the Department of Applied Economics, Cambridge University, and Professor John H. Dunning, of Reading University, for their kind help; and to Professor H. Lee Remmers, European Institute of Business Administration, Fontainebleau, whose contribution is fully annotated throughout the book.

Although all of the above provided indispensable assistance, it must be stated that the book conveys no conclusions or judgments other than my own.

W. A. P. MANSER

London

Introduction

(a) Scope of the Study

Along with other aspects of international companies' behaviour, that of their financial management has recently come under intensified scrutiny.

Understandably, some concern has been expressed, in both private and official quarters, regarding the impact which international companies' financial transactions may have upon the countries in which the latter operate. The question has been raised whether these operations are beneficial or detrimental to the balance of payments and to the domestic financial markets of individual countries. It is felt that in some cases the outward movement of investment capital, or alternatively, the remittance of profits and other investment proceeds, may place undue strain on the external payments position of countries affected. Similarly, it is wondered whether the export of capital by major international companies may not be too great a drain on the capital resources of the countries in which these companies are based. Equally, fears have been expressed that the financing operations of these companies in the host countries where they are installed may constitute an excessive claim on the capital resources of their hosts, both as regards the medium- and long-term securities market, and the provision of bank credit.

Finally, there is understandable interest in the procedures whereby the finances of international companies are managed. Does the world-wide posture and the integrated structure of these companies give them special financial advantages? Are their managers able to concentrate profits and funds in low taxation areas, or in areas of likely currency appreciation, or to borrow on more favourable terms than local national enterprises? For their part, the international companies themselves have inclined to the view that their operations, so far from overriding the national framework, are hampered by a multiplicity of requirements—on taxation, exchange control, development policy, company law, and other issues— to which they are exposed solely by reason of their international nature. On the impact of their transactions on national balances of payments and capital markets the international companies have been largely silent, being in the main ill-equipped with the economic data necessary for the discussion of the point.

The last statement highlights an important feature of the current discussion on the finances of international corporations. There is a dearth of systematic data on the subject.

The discussion as to the benefits or ill-effects which these companies bring has therefore had to be conducted on an inferential, rather than a factual, basis. This is particularly true of the effect on national balances of payments and capital markets. The supposed strains on, or contributions to, the latter have had to be discussed in the absence of collated evidence substantiating the argument one way or the other. The same is true, although perhaps to a lesser extent, of the question of international corporations' financial activities *vis-à-vis* national taxation, exchange control, and other requirements.

The present study therefore has a central purpose. This is to supply, as fully as possible, the factual data which has so far been absent. Analysis of published and unpublished material, collection of data from individual companies, and discussion both with officials and the financial managers of companies, has elucidated a body of evidence which may help to clarify the questions at issue. This material is presented in the following pages. It is stressed that the whole study treats only the financial aspect of international companies' behaviour.

The study is divided into two parts: I—Financial Dimensions; and II—Financial Management.

Part I—Financial Dimensions—will set out, as can best be computed, the physical size of the funds held and moved by international companies, and will show these in relation to the financial environment within which they operate; i.e. to total balance of payments flows and to the total generation and use of capital and credit in individual countries and regions. This section will divide itself naturally, in response to the issues now widely under discussion, into three parts:

1 Effect on balances of payments.
2 Effect on capital resources.
3 Effect on financial markets.

Part II—Financial Management—will consider the national requirements as to the use and movement of financial funds to which the financial managers of international companies are subject; the way in which the latter respond to these, and the effect of this response on the economic welfare of the countries concerned, and also of the companies themselves.

(b) Definitions

A number of interesting studies have recently attempted to define more exactly what is meant by the term 'international company'. Classifications according to geography—'international'; 'transnational', 'multinational'; 'supranational'—or, according to motivation—'ethnocentric'; 'polycentric'; 'geocentric'—and others, have been devised. For the purposes of the present study, it has been decided, after due reflection, not to adopt a definition such as these, for whatever practical use they may have in a number of aspects of international company activity, such as production policy, labour relations and management selection, they do not appear to have a bearing on the financial transactions of such companies. Companies operating internationally will necessarily export capital; reinvest earnings; remit dividends and loan interest; borrow and repay in international capital and money markets; issue shares in the home and host countries. Their effects on national and international financial aggregates will therefore be the same, whatever the particular category to which they may be said to belong. Indeed, an international company in any of the extreme forms indicated by some of the above-quoted definitions does not seem to exist, at least in the legal and financial sense. Save for a few well-established exceptions[1] all 'international enterprises' have one parent incorporated in one country only and subject to its exchange control, taxation and other legislation; and subsidiaries which are registered national companies of the host countries, subject to equivalent provisions. No company operating internationally can be held to be divorced, by its intrinsic nature, from the patterns of financial requirements of nations and states as a whole. In fact, for purposes of financial analysis, it is clear that the phenomenon involved is no more than that hitherto familiar under the title 'direct investment' i.e.: the financial flows induced by companies based in one country, but producing and selling in one or more other countries. For similar reasons, it has not been thought appropriate to restrict the concept of international companies to those having a minimum number of installations abroad. Again, there seems broadly no merit in concentrating attention on manufacturing or any other single type of international business.

What follows, therefore, is essentially a study of the phenomenon of 'direct investment'. It might be felt that this entails two drawbacks: one, that a number of small companies having a minimal commitment overseas, and certainly not entitled to the ranking of 'multinational enterprise', may be included; and two, that figures for companies involved in purely

---

[1] E.g. Royal Dutch/Shell and Unilever have each two parent companies, one parent being incorporated in the Netherlands and the other in the United Kingdom. Agfa/Gavaert has one parent company (itself a subsidiary of Farbenfabriken Bayer, Leverkusen) incorporated in Germany and the other in Belgium. Dunlop/Pirelli has one Dunlop parent company in the United Kingdom and an Italian and a Swiss parent company on the Pirelli side. The VFW/Fokker holding company, incorporated in Germany, is 50 per cent owned by the former German shareholders in VFW and 50 per cent by a Netherlands parent company. The majority of the French Citroën Company is owned by a holding company, parents of which are Michelin of France and Fiat of Italy.

A*

distributive activities abroad, may be included in the totals. The answer in both cases appears to be that the data for these two classes are both inseparable from, and very small in relation to, the main totals. Thus, if one assumes that only 20 per cent of the assets af the major American companies listed in the Fortune '500 List' are held abroad, then these assets amounted to some $85 billion in 1970 in comparison with a probable world total of $140 billion foreign-held assets.[2] Thus the share of small companies is bound to be small. Nor indeed is it necessarily desirable that investment in purely distributive activities should be entirely excluded. A degree of sales and merchandising infrastructure is inseparable from the process of manufacture in countries outside the home base. Such indications as are available suggest, in any case, that this forms a very small part of the total weight of direct investment abroad. United States data[3] shows assets of this sort to be only 8·2 per cent of total assets held abroad by United States companies. The equivalent figure for British direct investment overseas[4] is 15·1 per cent.

The ensuing study will therefore examine the financial impact of direct investment abroad of all kinds, by companies in all industries; it being implicit therein that the figures will effectively relate to the finances of major international companies in major industries. Where appropriate, it will however deal with the experiences of specific sectors.

It follows that the figures presented will be aggregates; they will not reflect the experiences of individual companies, which may vary considerably. They will none the less show the real effect on national balances of payments and capital markets, of the totality of international companies. Also, given that the aggregate figures will include the experience of small companies and of investment solely in distribution, they will tend to overstate the impact of the 'multinationals' properly speaking—an error, perhaps, on the right side.

[2] Viz UK and US 1970: $100 billion: see *Survey of Current Business*, October 1971, page 32, Table 6A, HMSO, *The United Kingdom Balance of Payments* 1971, Table 42 ('Direct' and 'Oil' assets): assumed to be 70 per cent of world total (see Table 1—Statistical Appendix).
[3] *Survey of Current Business*, 30th October 1970: 'The International Investment Position of the United States' Table 6.
[4] *Business Monitor M4*—Overseas Transactions—April 1971, Table 17.

PART I

Financial Dimensions

CHAPTER I

Effects on Balances of Payments

(a) Nature of Effects

The main impact on balances of payments consists of the export and reimport of capital by parent companies, and within company groups; and the transfer of income on this capital. 'Capital' comprises all financial resources, whether in the form of equity or loan capital supplied to subsidiaries, branches and associate companies abroad. 'Income' comprises returns on capital, i.e. all remittances of dividends (whether on Preferred or Ordinary shares), loan interest, and profits from branches. All these transactions come, for balance of payments purposes, under the generic heading of 'Long-Term Capital', i.e. capital intended for lasting use by the recipient. Short-term capital movements are also engendered by international companies, but these will be considered in Part II.

It is worth noting that there is a connection between the two main flows defined above, in that some profits and dividends are ploughed back into the overseas enterprise—or 'reinvested'. Reinvested earnings are thus a component both of 'income' and of 'capital', and are normally included on both sides of the account in official statistics. This point is mentioned pro memoria at this stage: it will not affect the material immediately following, but will be reverted to in due course.

A further item not included in the above two headings consists of management fees and royalties, but this will be taken into account at the appropriate stage.

The major repository of the above figures is the International Monetary Fund, which regularly publishes complete balance of payments figures on a uniform basis for most countries of the world. The DAC (Development Advisory Committee of the OECD) has also undertaken researches into the flows of capital and income between developed and less-developed countries. The present study is based primarily upon IMF returns—adjusted, where indicated, by the results of DAC researches.

It is worth noting at the outset that the task of compilation is a formidable one. Some one hundred separate countries are involved, displaying

multiple disparities in recording techniques and coverage. Although the
IMF and DAC have substantially resolved these manifold difficulties, it
must be borne in mind that the results produced, although reliable as
indications of the magnitudes involved, cannot offer a narrow degree of
precision.

(b) Size of Fund Movements

The first consideration is the total volume of finances moving under the
two headings. IMF data for the most recently recorded period—1964 to
1968 inclusive—show the following:

Total Outflow of Capital:	$35,153·3 m.
of which	
from Developed Countries	$35,100·0 m.
Less Developed Countries	$53·3 m.

The obverse of this flow, i.e. the inflow into individual countries of
direct investment capital, is also recorded by the IMF and is as follows for
the same period:

Total Inflows of Capital:	$32,465·0 m.
of which	
into Developed Countries[1]	$26,225·5 m.
Less Developed Countries	$6,239·5 m.

The above figures are net; i.e. they show outlays of capital less redemp-
tions.

Three major points immediately arise from the above table.

The first is, as might be supposed, that the outflow of direct investment
capital originates overwhelmingly from the developed, or industrialised,
countries. The proportion of capital exported by the developing countries
is so small as to be negligible.

The second major point is that the *destination* of capital flows lies
overwhelmingly in other developed countries. Of the total outflow of some
$35 billion, no less than 74 per cent, or $26 billion, went into other industrialised areas. Thus what is seen in the field of direct investment is not
so much a net capital outflow, as a cycling of capital around industrialised
countries as a whole.

The third point is that there is a clear asymmetry between total recorded
outflows and total recorded inflows, amounting to some $3 billion, and
that this appears to be at the expense of the less developed countries. The
latter report an inflow of some $6 billion, whereas subtraction of capital
receipts by developed countries from capital *exports* by the same countries

[1] This includes an inflow of $5,000 m. mainly from the United States of America not
published in the regular compilations, but stated by the IMF secretariat to be an estimated
total of reinvested earnings not recorded by the recipient countries.

—giving a residual which by definition should be the capital flow into less developed countries—produces a figure of some $9 billion. This point can, however, best be discussed after the figures for income have been considered.

IMF recordings for income for the same period (1964 to 1968) are as follows:

Total Investment Income received:	$42,208·1 m.
of which	
by Developed Countries	$41,994·1 m.
Less Developed Countries	$214·0 m.

In the same way as for capital, the IMF obtains the obverse returns; i.e. of investment income paid by individual countries. The totals are as follows:

Total Investment Income paid:	$42,827·6 m.
of which	
by Developed Countries	$22,888·4 m.[2]
Less Developed Countries	$19,939·2 m.

It will be seen from the above table that for practical purposes the whole of income receipts, and the bulk of income payments, are made by developed countries, as might be expected, given their lion's share of direct investment capital. These payments, again, are payments not lost by, but shared between, industrialised countries as a whole.

(c) *The Share of Developing Countries*

The apparent relative position of the developing countries must now be considered. It will be clear that on the basis of the returns made to the IMF, developing countries not only appear to receive a disproportionately small share of capital outflows ($6,000 m. out of $35,000 m.) but pay a substantial share of total investment income ($20,000 m. out of $43,000 m.).

This is a point of some significance, since as already stated, these are the figures officially published by the IMF. Within the immense global reconciliation effected by the latter body, it is of course a minor statistical misfit. However, within the purview of direct investment alone, it is of importance, and is no doubt duly noted by those concerned in developing countries. The impression of disproportionate receipts and payments is heightened by the fact that the payments apparently made by developing countries reflect a much larger return on assets held in their countries than on assets held in industrialised countries. According to the DAC, total asset stocks in industrialised countries amounted to $61,116 m. in 1966, whilst the equivalent stocks in less developed countries totalled

[2] Including the $5,000 m. of unreported reinvested earnings mentioned above (footnote to table on page 18).

$28,467 m. The above tabulation of income arisings suggests, therefore, an annual average yield of 7·5 per cent on assets in developed countries, and of 14·0 per cent in less developed countries.

At this point the researches undertaken by the DAC are of relevance. The DAC has conducted a number of separate enquiries into flows of capital and income between industrialised and developing countries, and the results do much to resolve the anomalies apparently arising from the above.

Firstly, the DAC has found that a proportion of the capital exports reported by developed countries are not reported as capital receipts by less developed countries. This is firstly because a certain amount of reinvested earnings are not included as capital receipts, particularly in a number of Latin American countries. Secondly, and more importantly, the total number of developing countries reporting to the IMF is markedly smaller than the number of developing countries to which industrialised countries' capital actually proceeds. Countries absent from the IMF returns in this way include Algeria, Kuwait, Malaysia, the Netherlands Antilles, most Francophone developing countries in Africa, Liberia, Uganda, Tanzania, the United Arab Republic, Syrian Arab Republic, Jordan, Abu Dhabi, Dubai, Singapore, Cambodia, Laos, Papua & New Guinea, and others.

The DAC has produced figures for exports of capital to less developed countries for the years 1964 to 1968 in which these gaps are filled. These can be compared with the capital receipts reported to the IMF, as follows:

Capital Receipts by Less Developed Countries

$m.	1964	1965	1966	1967	1968	Total
IMF	1,039	1,399	1,281	1,234	1,287	6,240
DAC	1,304	2,200	1,911	1,898	2,838	10,151

SOURCE: DAC—1971 Development Assistance Review. (Adjusted to the IMF definition of 'Less Developed Countries'; i.e. Table II–1 less data for Europe in Table VI–2: 1964 figure assumed to be the same as 1965/66). See also Table 2 in the Appendix.

It will be seen that the figure resulting from the DAC calculation ($10·2 m.) accords fairly closely with the residual obtained above from the IMF returns on capital exports to, and capital receipts by, the developed countries of some $9,000 m. It would therefore appear safe to say that the actual direct investment capital receipts of developing countries in the period 1964 to 1968 amounted to some $9–10,000 m.

Turning now to the figures for investment income payments, the DAC investigations again lead to different results from those reported to the IMF.[3] Thus for 1966, DAC estimates show total payments of profits, dividends and interest by developing countries of $2,912 m. This compares

[3] See Table 3 in the Appendix.

with the figure of $4,098·5 m. in the IMF statistics; it equals only 71 per cent of the latter.

This difference arises from a complicated variety of factors, but centres basically on the profits reported by the petroleum industry. As is known, the governments of crude oil producing countries have, for a variety of reasons, required petroleum companies to record profits as though sales proceeds were equal to the Posted Prices for exports of crude oil from those countries. In reality the crude oil is sold at prices substantially below (perhaps as much as 20 per cent[4]) these quotations. Consequently, officially reported profits have been much above those in fact achieved. The DAC's figure shown above is one derived from a recalculation of petroleum companies' profits, based on an assessment of their true yields in the various countries.

Applying the ratio between the DAC and IMF results for 1966 to the full IMF data for the period 1964 to 1968, a figure for investment income payments by less developed countries emerges as follows:

$$\frac{\$19,939\cdot2 \text{ m.}}{100} \times 71 = \$14,156\cdot8 \text{ m.}$$

This appears to be a reliable adjustment. The reduction in developing countries' outgoings (of $5,782·4 m.) must, of course, also be applied to total receipts of investment income reported by developed countries, bringing these down from the $41,994·1 m. quoted above to $36,211·7 m. If the investment income outgoings of developed countries themselves ($22,888·4 m.) is subtracted from this, the balance, $13,323·3 m.—which by definition is the investment income derived from developing countries— is very close to the figure computed above.

In the light of all the above considerations, it is now possible to put together a revised table of capital and income movements for the world as a whole, which is internally consistent. Given the inevitable margins of error in figures of this compass, it is appropriate at this stage to express the total in billions of dollars:

Capital Outflows

From Developed Countries	$35·1 b.[5]
Less Developed Countries	0·1 b.
Total	$35·2 b.

[4] Since the period under review (1964–68) the Teheran Agreement and other developments have increased the margin well beyond 20 per cent.
[5] In theory this figure should be reduced by the element of reinvested earnings contained in the income from developing countries which have been subtracted: this would be about $2 billion. However, for a number of reasons arising out of the approximate nature of the magnitudes involved, this does not seem desirable. There is good reason to suppose that the figure for the total capital outflows of developed countries is an underestimate. For instance, the IMF data does not include UK oil investment outflows
[*continued on next page*]

Capital Inflows
>   Into Developed Countries $26·2 b.
>   Less Developed Countries   9·5 b.
>   _____
>   *Total* $35·7 b.

Investment Income Received
>   By Developed Countries $36·2 b.
>   Less Developed Countries   0·2 b.
>   _____
>   *Total* $36·4 b.

Investment Income Paid
>   By Developed Countries $22·9 b.
>   Less Developed Countries $13·7 b.
>   _____
>   *Total* $36·6 b.

The global picture presented by the above table can now be summarised. As will be seen, developed countries sent $35·1 billion of investment capital abroad, of which some $26·2 billion was destined to each other. Thus the true balance of payments outflow from these countries as a whole was $9·5 billion, which went to developing countries. At the same time, developed countries received $36·2 billion income, thus offsetting exactly their outlay of capital. For the group as a whole, the net outflow of capital ($9·5 billion) was counterbalanced by a net inflow of income of $13·7 billion.

It follows, of course, that developing countries' capital receipts, at some $9·5 billion, remained inferior to their income payments, at some $13·7 billion. Returns on capital assets also appear to be 9·9 per cent in developing countries as against 7·8 per cent in developed countries.

However, at this point the effect of petroleum industry flows must again be recalled. Despite the allowance made for the inflation of petroleum companies' earnings in less developed countries (see above) it remains true that the tax policies of the producing countries compel oil companies to concentrate their profits in those countries. Thus, in the case of the United States, accounting for 62·5 per cent of all world oil assets, if the corrected income arisings suggested by DAC are applied, then earnings in

[continued from previous page]
(presently some $1·3 billion for the period 1964–68) although receipts of UK oil investment capital are recorded by the DAC for developing countries and by the recipient industrialised countries. Other omissions, particularly in respect of reinvested earnings in developed countries, are possible. Again, income outflows from developing countries may be slightly underestimated owing to the reporting of some of these under 'other investment income' (i.e. portfolio and real estate and other investment income). (See 'Asymmetries and Errors in Reported Balance of Payments Statistics': John S. Smith, Assistant Director, Balance of Payments Division, IMF; and 'Problems of Measuring Private Capital Flows to Less Developed Countries: Report to the Development Assistance Committee of a Group of Experts'.) Probably the real flows of both capital and income balance out at levels slightly higher than those shown above. All in all, however, it seems best to maintain the figures as tabulated as the best median guide to the real flows.

developing countries in 1966 still amounted to $760 m.[6] as against $155 m.[7] in developed countries, although US oil assets were distributed in that year in the proportion of 53 per cent to 47 per cent in favour of the developed countries.[8]

The relatively high oil income returns from the developing countries thus remain a fact. However, as stated above, this appears to be the choice of the producing countries' governments themselves. This statement is not meant to imply that producing countries' governments are solely responsible for the concentration of petroleum profits in their territories. Oil companies might well have been happy (particularly in the period shortly after the war) to raise the price of refined products and reduce that of crude. However, they collided at this point with the desire of a number of governments, particularly in Western Europe, to safeguard indigenous fuel industries, which expressed itself in the imposition of heavy fuel oil duties. This discouraged a further rise in the prices of refined products. By this time also, oil companies were already committed to sizeable tax contributions to producing-country governments, who naturally disapproved of any plans for a reduction of the profit accruals to which these applied. Oil profit sources therefore became immobilised in producing countries through the insistence of the producer governments on the one hand and the tacit consent of the consumer governments on the other.

In an earlier period still, before the Second World War, oil companies were still struggling for a share of the energy market, and this resulted in downward pressure on the prices of their refined products. At the same time, investment costs of exploration and extraction were, given the stage of development of the industry, significantly higher than those of marketing and distribution, thus again implying a need for a higher return in producer than in consumer countries.

All in all, events over the years appear to have conspired to concentrate oil profits in producing countries. It could, of course, be argued that the oil companies might have relied more on external funds than on internally generated capital, but apart from the probable inability of the international capital market—until recent years—to provide sums of the magnitude involved, the combined taxation policies of consumer and producer countries would still have driven oil profits into the latter, and presumably at undiminished volume.

If oil is excluded entirely from the calculations, then the following is the position for the US and the UK for the period 1964–1968. (These two countries accounted for $52 billion[9] of the world total of non-petroleum assets of $63·6 billion[10] in 1966.)

[6] 10 per cent of value of assets in developing countries as shown in *Survey of Current Business*, October 1970. (For the assumed yield see DAC (68) 14 of 23rd April, 1968).
[7] *Survey of Current Business*, October 1970.
[8] *Ibid.*
[9] *Survey of Current Business*, October 1970. UK *Balance of Payments* HMSO 1971.
[10] DAC (68) 14.

Capital Outflows[11]

	$b.
To Developed Countries	12·0
Developing Countries	3·2
Total	15·2

Income

	$b.
From Developed Countries[12]	17·0
Developing Countries	5·8
Total	22·8

A clear picture arises from the above table. The bias in the figures resulting from the high capital flows to developed and developing countries for oil investment, combined with low petroleum investment income from developed countries and high petroleum investment income from developing countries, has been removed. It will be seen that to both classes of countries, capital outflows from the US and the UK are accompanied by considerably greater income inflows.

An important point is to be drawn from this tabulation, and one that suggests an overall balance of payments benefit of continued direct investment activity. A situation in which investment returns exceed current capital exports appears to be the norm. This arises essentially from the nature of industrial enterprise. A manufacturing or other producing installation, once set up by the use of original capital, will proceed to expand, and in particular, to increase its fixed assets, mainly through the medium of its internally-generated capital, or its cash flow (retained profits plus provisions for depreciation). This is true of all enterprise, whether confined within the domestic boundaries of individual countries, or whether resulting from direct investment abroad. The cash flow element in the total sources of funds of domestic-based industry constitutes in industrialised countries a percentage of some 60–70 per cent. The same is true, as will be shown in Chapter 3 below, of the subsidiaries of international companies. In addition, the expanding enterprise is increasingly able to incorporate a fixed-interest loan element into its capital structure (this loan capital may well be raised locally by the subsidiaries of international companies, although this is more likely in developed than in developing countries, as will be shown later). The result of all this is that as time passes the flow of profits derives increasingly from these other sources of funds, rather than from the input of new equity capital. This means that in terms of international companies, the return flow of profits will become larger, in any given year, than the input of fresh capital by the parent company. In balance of payments terms, this leads to the

---

[11] *Survey of Current Business*, October 1970, page 31, Table 9: 'Net Capital Outflows.' *Business Monitor M4*—Tables 16 and 21.
[12] Including $5,000 m. of unreported earnings.

high income outflow/low capital inflow situation illustrated in the table above.

Developing countries should not, therefore, attach undue significance to the fact that investment income outgoings appear to exceed new capital input. In this respect developing countries are in the same position as developed countries, and the balance of payments effects constitute the premium, probably low, required for the economic advantages of the installation of new economic enterprise within their borders. An historical reference is perhaps of assistance in this context. It has recently been pointed out[13] that 'although the net stock of us foreign indebtedness rose from $200 m. in 1843 to $3,700 m. in 1914, net payments of interest and dividends amounted to $5,800 m. in the same period'. Professor Dunning comments that it would be erroneous not to set against these figures the managerial and technological impetus given to the American economy as a whole by this foreign enterprise. The subsequent history of the United States, which has now developed both into the largest of the world economies, and the largest international investor, appears to substantiate Professor Dunning's point. What is missing from the balance of payments position of the developing countries is of course the obverse of inward direct investment—outward direct investment—which the developed countries have, and which balances their external flows. With the expansion of the developing countries' economies, this effect should take increasing shape.[14]

However there are, in the above figures, elements calling for the sounding of a mildly precautionary note. The income receipts noted from developing countries are, in proportion to capital flows, appreciably higher than those shown for developed countries. There may be a number of reasons for this. At the outset, however, it must be stated that the difference does not appear to derive from a pursuit by international companies of higher earnings in relation to assets in developing countries than in developed countries. Figures estimated by the DAC for 1966[15] show that returns on non-oil assets were approximately the same in both categories of countries. The British Department of Trade & Industry[16] estimates

---

[13] Professor J. H. Dunning: *Studies in International Investment*, George Allen & Unwin, 1970—page 171.

[14] In a few oil-producing countries there is already a growing outflow of capital.

[15] DAC (68) 14 (Tables 8, 9 and 15)

	$m.
Total non-oil assets in Less Developed Countries outside Europe in 1966	16,911
Total Earnings	1,744
Yield 10·3 per cent	
Total non-oil assets in Developed Countries in 1966	46,730
Total Earnings (estimated on basis of us/uk weighting)	4,400
Yield 9·4 per cent	

[16] *Business Monitor*, HMSO Series M4—Table 37.

that in the years 1965–68 yields on direct investment non-oil assets in less developed countries averaged 8·9 per cent, whilst those in developed countries averaged 8·5 per cent. United States Department of Commerce[17] data show that yields on the United States non-oil assets in developed countries averaged 10·4 per cent in the years 1964–68, as against a yield of some 9·1 per cent in the same period for assets in less developed countries.

The earnings element being therefore identical for both developed and developing countries, the only explanation for the difference in the two flows must be that fresh capital input into subsidiaries in developing countries is lower than that into subsidiaries in industrialised countries. This can be easily demonstrated on the figures:

United States Capital Outflows

$m.	1950–59	1960–69
Total Capital Outflow	11,152	25,776
of which to LDCs	4,173	6,492
% to LDCs	37·4%	25·2%
LDCs		
Latin America	3,201	
Africa	267	
Asia	705	
Total	4,173	

SOURCE: US Department of Commerce Balance of Payments Statistical Supplement 1963, Revised Edition. *Survey of Current Business*, October 1970.

United States Direct Investment Assets Abroad

$m.	1950	1959	% Growth 1950–59	1960	1969	% Growth 1960–69
In all Countries	11,788	29,805	152·8	31,865	70,763	122·0
In LDCs	6,275	13,430	114·0	12,546	23,060	83·8

SOURCE: 1950–59: *Survey of Current Business*, August 1961. 1960–69: *Survey of Current Business*, October 1970.

Thus, in the two periods compared, both the rate of capital input from the United States into developing countries, and the growth of assets, has been slower in the second period than in the first. Similar results are ascertainable from UK data.

UK Direct Investment

£m.	1963	1968
Total Capital Outflows	236	410
of which to LDCs	54	66
% to LDCs	22·9%	16·1%

SOURCE: *Business Monitor*, HMSO Series M4—Table 16.

[17] *Survey of Current Business*, October 1970—page 31, Table 9. (See Table 4 in the Statistical Appendix.)

UK Direct Investment Assets

£m.	1962	1968
Total Assets	3,405	5,585
In Developing Countries	1,274	1,668
% in Developing Countries	37·4%	29·9%

SOURCE: *Business Monitor,* HMSO Series M4—Table 34.

There has thus been a clear switch from developing to developed countries as investment destinations. It should of course be stressed that this is a relative move only. The absolute build-up of funds in developing countries has, as the figures show, progressed substantially. International companies, however, whilst continuing to invest in developing countries, have allocated even larger sums of capital to developed countries.

It remains to be considered why these differing trends have emerged. It could perhaps be wondered whether some investment assets in developing countries, such as those in the mining industry, are now fully worked up and require no further capital input. However, the share of mining in total investment in developing countries (9·7 per cent in 1966[18]) is not large enough to affect the overall figure in this way. Moreover, if this were the case, then an increase in earnings on assets should be expected, which is not, as the foregoing data shows, the case. Moreover, there are a number of investments of long maturity in developed countries (e.g. mining 6·5 per cent[18]), where the same capital input effect has not occurred.

A conclusion which remains open for consideration is that the economic opportunities offered, and the conditions imposed on foreign investment, are such as to make developed countries more attractive to international companies than developing countries. In the context of the present study, this possibility cannot be pursued further. However, it seems clear that the governments of developing countries might usefully consider whether the rate of economic expansion, and the encouragement offered to foreign investors in their countries, is suitable to maintain the rate of flow of direct investment capital into their industries.

(d) Direct Investment Flows in the Total Balance of Payments

The most important aspect—that of the relationship of flows on direct investment to the total flows in the balance of payments of the countries concerned—now remains to be considered.

At this point, it seems correct to take into account the effect of reinvestment of profits. As was stated earlier, these form a component both of income and of capital: i.e. they are income not in fact removed from the host country in which they are earned, and are thus described in the official statistics both as 'capital' and as 'income', and are incorporated in the

[18] DAC (68) 14. Adjusted for Europe.

figures on both sides of the account. It could be argued that the arrangement is best left in this form, since earnings retained in the host country are undoubtedly new acquisitions of capital by the country of the parent company, and are at the same time, in the year in which they arise, inindubitably income attributable to the country of the parent company. Moreover, the two flows are not in every sense distinguishable. Retained earnings may well take the place of a capital outflow from the parent company which would otherwise have occurred, and vice versa. On the other hand, it can well be maintained that since reinvested earnings do not, in fact, cross national frontiers, they are eliminated as a source of pressure on the actual balance of payments of the individual countries, and should therefore be subtracted when balance of payments issues pure and simple are being examined. For the latter reason it has been decided to reduce direct investment flows by the amount of reinvested earnings, for present purposes.

Very little hard evidence is available as to the proportion of income which is in fact reinvested. However, data is available for British and United States earnings, and a reasonably secure estimate can be made on the basis of these.[19] From this it is possible to deduce that the total of reinvested earnings is as follows:

Total Earnings and Reinvested Earnings in Developed and Developing Countries 1964–68

$ bn.	Total Earnings	Reinvested Earnings
Developing Countries	13·7	2·7
Developed Countries	22·9	10·5

(Here again, the heavy bias introduced by the reinvestment policies of oil companies is evident. Oil company earnings in producer countries are for the greater part remitted.)

With these figures it is now possible to construct a table showing the place occupied by direct investment flows in the total balance of payments flows of both developed and developing countries. The reinvested earnings element will, of course, be subtracted both on the capital and the income side.

The following two tables illustrate this for developing and for developed countries. As will be seen, they show the position occupied by direct investment flows in the total balance of payments flows of the countries concerned; i.e. they show the size of direct investment movements, compared with the total inward and outward movements of funds on account of transactions in goods and services, including transfers and government payments and on long-term capital as a whole.

[19] See Table 5 in the Statistical Appendix.

Direct Investment Flows in the Total Balance of Payments of Developing Countries—1964–68

	$000 *m.*
(1) Imports of Goods and Services[20]	−226·5
(2) Exports of Goods and Services[20]	+215·0
(3) Long-term Capital Outflow[21]	−18·6
(4) Long-term Capital Inflow[21]	+33·3
(5) Total Outflows (Items 1+3)	−245·1
(6) Total Inflows (Items 2+4)	+248·3
of which	
(7) Direct Investment Outflow	−11·1
(8) Direct Investment Inflow	+7·0
Direct Investment Flows as a percentage of Total Flows	
(9) Outflow	4·5
(10) Inflow	2·8

SOURCE: IMF. (Direct investment flows on DAC corrected basis with allowance for reinvested earnings.)

Direct Investment Flows in the Total Balance of Payments of Developed Countries—1964–68

	$000 *m.*
(1) Imports of Goods and Services[22]	−979·1
(2) Exports of Goods and Services[22]	+1,000·2
(3) Long-term Capital Outflow[23]	−59·6
(4) Long-term Capital Inflow[23]	+47·2
(5) Total Outflows (Items 1+3)	−1,038·7
(6) Total Inflows (Items 2+4)	+1,047·4
of which	
(7) Total Direct Investment Outflow[24]	−34·2
(8) Total Investment Inflow[25]	+38·3
Direct Investment Flows as a percentage of Total Flows	
(9) Outflow	3·3
(10) Inflow	3·7

SOURCE: IMF. (Direct investment flows throughout amended on DAC basis and reduced by amount of reinvested earnings.)

These tables serve to set the cross-frontier financial movements of international companies in perspective, and they are instructive. As will

---

[20] Including transfers, government transactions and all investment income flows.
[21] Including government capital flows and all investment flows.
[22] Including transfers, government transactions and all investment income flows.
[23] Including government capital flows and all investment flows.
[24] Sum of capital exports and income payments. (See also Table 11 in the Appendix.)
[25] Sum of capital imports and income receipts. (See also Table 11 in the Appendix.)
See also Tables 6–12 in the Appendix.

be seen, the size of these movements in relation to the total flows across the balances of payments of the countries concerned is small. This applies both to developed and to developing countries. Total outflows of funds on direct investment account in developing countries in the period under examination were 4·5 per cent of the overall balance of payments outflows of these countries, whilst total inflows accounted for 2·8 per cent of the whole in the case of developed countries, the percentages were 3·3 per cent and 3·7 per cent respectively.

The further tables in the Statistical Appendix show more detailed data for individual regions and countries, both in the developed and in the developing areas of the world.[26]

(e) The International Money and Capital Market

The use by international companies of purely international sources of funds for their financial operations has a bearing on balance of payments matters which is worthy of examination. The purely international sources to which reference is here intended are the so-called 'Eurocurrency' and 'Eurobond' markets, and the lending of international financial institutions. By the 'Euro-currency' market is meant the borrowing of funds denominated in a particular currency, but held by a non-resident bank as a claim on a bank in the country concerned. By the Eurobond market is meant the financing of bonds, normally issued through international syndicates, from the non-resident funds described above, or the issue of bonds in those centres where exchange controls permit the expatriation of the proceeds of such issues. These two categories represent in effect two international capital markets, at medium- and long-term, and loans in them are often designated as 'international' and 'traditional foreign bond issues'. By international financial institutions is meant the various public international banking institutions such as the International Bank for Reconstruction & Development; the International Development Association; the International Finance Corporation; ADELA; the various regional Development Banks set up by the countries in the areas concerned, and other official bodies whose function is to dispense funds recruited internationally.

The balance of payments effect of recourse to these funds will be treated according to the three main types of funds: Eurocurrencies, Eurobonds, and the funds of international institutions.

Taking first Eurocurrencies: the funds may be borrowed by the parent company, either direct or through the medium of financial subsidiaries

---

[26] It will be noted from these tables that the United States alone of developed countries had a balance of payments outflow marginally higher than the inflow. This may be due more to the vagaries of the period chosen, in which capital exports were very high ($3,123 m. annually in 1964–68 as against $1,726 m. in 1960–63)—thus unduly weighting the equation—than to any long-term structural effect.

abroad, and allocated to its foreign affiliates; money borrowed abroad by the parent and imported into its own country will not normally be re-exported for use by foreign subsidiaries, and if used for domestic purposes by the parent company, it falls out of the province of the present study. Funds may also be borrowed by the foreign affiliates of the international company, either direct, or through the intermediary of the group's financial subsidiaries in other countries. The balance of payments effects of these two forms of operation may now be defined in turn. Eurocurrency funds recruited direct or through financial intermediaries by parent companies, and reassigned to foreign affiliates, constitute an actual import of capital into the countries of the affiliate, and are so recorded in the balance of payments accounts of those countries. As regards the countries of the parent companies: these funds are looked upon by the balance of payments authorities, rightly, as an outward direct investment flow, and are so recorded. The capital funds employed are thus recorded as a debit item in the parent country's balance of payments. However, as already stated, the funds in question derive from international sources outside the physical balance of payments flows of the parent country. Funds borrowed in the name of the subsidiary are an import of capital into the host country, but do not register as an export of capital from the parent country.

Funds raised by Eurobond issues, again, constitute a real capital import into the host country. Where they are a traditional foreign bond issue—whether the fund-raising party is a foreign parent company, a foreign operating subsidiary, or a foreign financial subsidiary—they are a real outflow of funds from the country of the currency concerned. Since they are funds transmitted from those countries as financial assets, and not as the investment capital of resident companies, they are, logically, not shown in the direct investment section of the balance of payments account of that country, although they do appear in another part of the balance of payments tables.

As regards the country of the parent company, a book outflow of investment capital is recorded, as in the case of Eurocurrency borrowings, although no physical funds leave the territory of that country. However, an important exception to this rule is the United States, which does not count overseas-issued Eurobonds as United States capital outflows.

Where the fund-raiser is an operating subsidiary itself—although these cases are rare—the funds so raised are not shown as a capital export of the parent country.

Where a true international issue is involved, then a real capital import accrues to the host country, and where the fund-raiser is the parent (outside the USA) a capital export is registered in the balance of payments accounts of the parent country, although in fact no draw is made upon the capital of that country. Where—in rare cases—the subsidiary issues the bond, a true capital import occurs, but no concurrent capital export of the parent country is recorded.

In short, then, the sum effect of all of the above is as follows. Where true Euro-funds are procured by the parent company, a real inward flow of capital into the host country is set up, and is duly recorded; a book outflow of capital from the parent country is recorded (except from the USA), but in fact the real source of the funds is the international market lying outside the balance of payments of the parent country, and the balance of payments of that country suffers in the event no diminution by reason of this transaction. Where 'traditional foreign bond issues' are made by the parent company, the host country receives a true capital import; the country of the loan currency records a true portfolio investment outflow; but the parent country (except the USA) records a purely book outflow of direct investment capital. The result, for the purposes of this study, is that a proportion of those flows deemed 'capital outflows' for direct investment by parent countries is not in fact such, and the balance of payments impact calculated in the earlier pages above may be diminished accordingly.

The function of international financial institutions may be dealt with more summarily. The overwhelming proportion of these institutions are intergovernmental bodies collecting funds for supply to member and other governments. Such institutions as exist which may be deemed to be private perform functions no different from the private financial institutions in the banking centres referred to above, and the effect of their operations has accordingly been covered by the above analysis. Since the official international financial institutions' funds are used by recipient governments often for industrial investment purposes, the total amount distributed is of interest as a measure of comparison with the private international flows in being, and this will be estimated below.

Finally in this context—although the raising of funds is not involved—there is some point in referring to the fairly common use of international financial subsidiaries for the sole purpose of assembling funds derived from various international sources, and redistributing these to other members of the international company group. The flows involved are entered in the balance of payments account of the countries concerned—such as the Netherlands Antilles—but not in the section devoted to direct investment. However, these flows are necessarily self-cancelling and although the operation will merit further mention later, it needs no further attention from the point of view of the balance of payments.

The above states the position regarding capital flows. However, these capital contributions raise a counterflow consisting of capital and interest repayments, which must be taken into account in establishing the full effect on balances of payments. These repayments constitute a real balance of payments outflow in the host countries, and are so recorded.

Having been paid out, however, these flows are used for the servicing and redemption of the Euro-fund loans. This then, from the point of view of the parent country, completes a financial circuit which lies in its entirety outside the parent country's balance of payments. As before, where traditional foreign issues are concerned, the payments go back to the country of issue and are, again, recorded in the 'portfolio investment' section of the relevant balance of payments accounts.

To recapitulate all of the above: Euro-funding of direct investment produces a real and recorded inflow of capital and outflow of capital and income from host countries; it produces corresponding flows of capital and income in the international markets lying outside the parent, or indeed any other country's balance of payments, except in the sole case of traditional foreign issues. It is recorded, none the less, as outflows in the 'direct investment' section of the balance of payments of many parent countries.

It remains now to quantify as far as is possible the flows involved, and their impact upon individual countries' balances of payments. To take first the Eurocurrency market: the size of this source of funds is clearly the change in total liabilities between the beginning and the end of the period in question. Total Eurodollar[27] liabilities, according to the Bank for International Settlements,[28] rose from $9,000 m. in December 1964 to $25,000 m. in December 1968—an increase of $16,000 m. However, it would clearly be erroneous to assume that the whole of this large borrowing of funds was the work solely of international companies, and that the direct investment outflow of $35,000 m. recorded on page 21 for the 1964–68 period should be reduced accordingly. Eurodollar funds are procured by various other parties, including national companies operating solely within their country borders, and central governments and municipal authorities; the personal sector also has a significant share in total Eurocurrency operations, as does the banking sector for purely banking purposes. The problem therefore is to identify that part of the Eurocurrency market which is occupied by the international companies themselves.

Information on this point is relatively scanty. For the UK, some precise and valuable data is provided by the United Kingdom authorities in the annual *United Kingdom Balance of Payments*[29] These records show that in the years 1965 to 1969 inclusive, the Eurocurrency borrowing by UK parent companies for the purpose of direct investment abroad amounted to £161 m. ($451 m. at 1964 exchange rates), or an average of $90 m. per year. This compares with an average direct investment outflow

---

[27] Figures for other currencies were unimportant until 1970.
[28] 39th Annual Report, 1968-1969, page 149.
[29] HMSO: *The United Kingdom Balance of Payments*, 1969, 1970, 1971; Annex 4, Table 'Financing of Direct Investment Cash Transactions in the Sterling Area'.

of $1,017 m. annually over the quinquennium 1964–68, suggesting that some 9 per cent of foreign capital investment—registered as physical fund outflows from the United Kingdom—were in fact financed from international sources, and did not constitute a charge on the United Kingdom balance of payments.

Figures are unfortunately not available for other countries; this is perhaps particularly regrettable in the case of the United States, whose international companies are reputed to operate comparatively heavily in the Eurocurrency market. However, given that those capital export restrictions which encourage companies to resort to the international money market are not weightier in the United Kingdom than in other major capital-exporting countries, it may be safe to assume that the proportion of direct investment financed by Eurocurrency borrowing was, for the world as a whole, not less than that for the United Kingdom. This would suggest, therefore, that of the total of $35,000 m. recorded for world direct investment outflows for 1964–68, some $3,200 m. derived from Eurocurrency sources rather than from national balance of payments sources. This represents some 20 per cent of the total Eurocurrency market of $16,000 m. mentioned above.

As regards Eurobond funding, information is available from a number of sources, including primarily the IBRD[30] and the Bank for International Settlements. The former has listed all issues by borrower for the period 1960–69. Analysis of this suggests that international companies obtained some $7,300 m. from this market in the quinquennium 1964–68, or $1,460 m. annually.

It is of interest also to aggregate the balance of payments data available on the subject for the US and the UK. The United States Department of Commerce *Survey of Current Business* for October 1970[31] shows total foreign bond issues by United States corporations at $4,686 m. in the quinquennium 1965–69 inclusive,[32] or $937 m. on an annual basis. For the United Kingdom, the *United Kingdom Balance of Payments*[33] shows 'direct borrowing abroad by parent companies' at $93 m. on an annual basis (at 1964 exchange rates). To this must be added figures published by the British Department of Trade and Industry[34] for borrowing abroad on behalf of UK parent companies by financial subsidiaries overseas amounting to some $48 m. annually. It would be prudent to assume

[30] *Chronological list of Foreign and International Bonds*, 1960–1969: by IBRD Economic and Social Data Division, Economic Program Department, August 1971.
[31] Page 36, Table 15.
[32] Total for 1965 assumed to be double the half-year total shown.
[33] HMSO: *The United Kingdom Balance of Payments*, 1969, 1970, 1971; Annex 4, Table 'Financing of Direct Investment Cash Transactions in the Sterling Area'.
[34] Trade and Industry, 7th April, 1971: page 31, Table 3. Figures are in fact shown only for 1968 and 1969, owing to the absence of earlier coverage. The annual average total for 1964–68 has been assumed to be £20 m. (for 1968 and 1969, borrowing in fact amounted to £25 m. and $32 m. respectively).

that half of this amount was in fact used by the parent in the UK. The sum total of Eurobond borrowing by British international companies would therefore be approximately $117 m. annually.

Aggregating the United States and the United Kingdom figures, it appears that of a total recorded direct investment outflow by the two countries of $5,611 m. annually in the period 1964–68, some $1,054 m. was procured by issues in the foreign and international bond market, or 19 per cent. Assuming this to be true of international companies as a whole, then it would follow that some $7,000 m. in the 1964–68 period derived from the international bond market—and this is indeed borne out by the actual data for international bond issues collected by the OECD, as shown above.

It remains to be seen how far this usage by international companies constituted a claim on the total international bond market. According to the Bank for International Settlements, 'foreign and international bond issues'[35] amounted to $18,861 m. for the quinquennium 1964–68, or an annual average of $3,772 m. The aggregate usage of international bond issues by international companies over the quinquennium—of $7,300 m., or $1,460 m. annually—therefore amounted to some 39 per cent of the total.

Finally, it follows from the above that the figure of $35,000 m. for world capital exports over the period 1964–68 should be reduced by some $5,500 m. if the true total for the export of capital by international companies across national balances of payments is to be stated. The sum of $5,500 m. is made up of the $3,200 m. borrowed on the Eurocurrency market, and of $2,300 m. ($7,000 m. – $4,700 m.) borrowed by non-US parent companies in the Eurobond market.

This figure is confirmed by the inferences which may be drawn from the UK experience which, as mentioned above, is recorded in full for both Eurocurrency and Eurobond operations. It will be seen that out of total recorded direct investment outflows of $1,070 m. annual average over 1964–68, some $207 m. derived from these two international markets. This represents 20 per cent of the total recorded balance of payments outflow. If this case is typical, then only some $28,000 m. of the $35,000 m. direct investment outflow recorded for the world in fact constituted a claim on the balance of payments resources of the capital-exporting countries in question.

(*f*) *Management Fees and Royalties*

To complete the analysis of the balance of payments position, it remains only to consider the role of management fees and royalties. These are the

[35] Bank for International Settlements Annual Report: 38th Annual Report for 1964, 1965, 1966; 41st Annual Report for 1967, 1968. The OECD Financial Statistics show a closely similar total—$20,376 m.

charges made by parent companies for their foreign subsidiaries' use of processes patented by the parent company, and for managerial and similar services supplied by the parent company against payment.

Such transactions, constituting as they do payment for services rendered, do not strictly speaking come within the purview of an examination solely of the financial flows of international companies. These flows, strictly defined, limit themselves to movements of capital and of income on that capital, in all the forms which these movements can take. They do not include payments on operating transactions such as the settlement of invoices for goods and services, which themselves predetermine the levels of eventual income on capital. Management fees and royalties do not, therefore, any more than payments for the sale of goods, figure in the IMF data for income on direct investment; nor do they of course occur in the relevant item of national balances of payments.

However, it is a fact that the payment of management fees and royalties is invariably referred to in those balance of payments publications of the US and the UK which relate to the financing of direct investment abroad. Moreover these payments can, in principle, be used as a substitute vehicle for the transfer of income itself; this will be described and considered in fuller detail in Part (II) of the present study.

For the above reasons it appears suitable to deal briefly, at this point, with the quantitative aspect of management fees and royalties.

Data on this subject is incomplete. However, the United States Department of Commerce shows total income by United States-based companies of $5,092 m. over the period 1964–68. The British Department of Trade and Industry show total receipts of $221 m. for the year 1969 alone. The United States Department of Commerce does not appear to have figures for outflows of royalty and service payments by US subsidiaries of foreign-owned companies, but it will be clear from the United Kingdom figures that these outflows could be substantial.

As regards the breakdown of royalty and fee-earnings between categories of countries, the US Department of Commerce shows figures for 1964, 1968 and 1969 which suggest that about 38 per cent of proceeds come from developing countries. The figures published by the Department of Trade and Industry of the United Kingdom indicate an almost identical share (41 per cent).

British statistics show outflows of royalties and fees of $31 m. in 1969. All in all, it is likely that these payments, taken for industrialised countries as a whole, are virtually self-balancing.

In relation to direct investment as a whole, royalty and fee revenues are not insubstantial. The American total of $5,000 m. compares with total earnings of some $24,000 m.; i.e. around 20 per cent. British receipts appear to be much less: about 4 per cent.

However, in the context of the overall balance of payments flows as shown in the preceding tables, the addition of these sums could not materially affect the percentages involved.

(g) *Conclusions on Balance of Payments Effects*

The first conclusion appears to be that it would be inadvisable to over-state the effects, either adverse or beneficial, of the financial flows of international companies on the balances of payments of the countries concerned. The volume of these flows is too small in relation to the total inflows and outflows across the exchanges to have a significant bearing on the overall external accounts of the countries.

A second main conclusion must be that direct investment flows, how-ever small in relation to the aggregate flows, are positive for the capital exporter. This derives from the inherent nature of business, whether it be domestic or international, which, once established, draws increasingly on internally-generated funds for the payment of profits, and thus decreasingly on new capital investment. Normally—that is to say, over the major part of the world investment spectrum—the profitability of outward capital flows is matched by that of inward capital flows. Where there is not a balance of inward and outward investment, as in the case of the developing countries, then one side of the equation operates. For reasons already explained, it cannot be concluded from this that discrimination is being exercised against developing countries, or that the proper interest of these countries lies in stemming existing capital inflows rather than impelling their economies onward to the point where equivalent capital exports can be mounted. Experience and historical precedent show that abundant, or indeed massive, inward investment is less of an obstacle than a stimulus, or an essential prerequisite, to economic expansion and outward investment in its turn. It should also be remembered that the balance of investment income payments and capital receipts in developing countries is also, it should be recalled, heavily biased by the profit policy imposed upon the oil industry. Finally, it has to be considered whether this ratio has been further biased by the different host climate offered foreign investors in developed and develop-ing countries.

Thirdly, and arising out of the above, it must be concluded that as far as industrialised countries are concerned, the balance of payments effects are largely neutral, since outflows from industrialised countries go into other industrialised countries. It is apparent, therefore, that in this domain industrialised countries are interdependent. Insofar as the capital inflows and income payments of industrialised countries are also their capital outflows and income receipts, these countries are at the same time, and in the same degree, both creditors and debtors on foreign assets held at home, and on their own assets held abroad. The governments of developed countries might well, therefore, bear in mind that official action *vis-à-vis* direct investment will always have a double effect. It will operate both on the balance of payments of other countries and on their own. Encouragement of direct investment will assist the balance of payments of foreign countries, but will also assist their own. Contrarily, discouragement of direct investment will injure the balance of payments of other countries and also their own.

It is of course true that at the moment the major share of direct investment flows is centred in the United States. However, it might be unwise to draw long-term conclusions from the present state of affairs, which has in fact lasted only since the Second World War. Prior to that date, flows from Europe to America were as great as those in the reverse direction. With the expansion and integration of the European economy now taking place, there are already signs of a revival of European direct investment abroad, and it is to be supposed that this will continue in the future.

CHAPTER 2

Effect on Capital Resources

The next issue for examination is the effect of international companies' operations on the capital resources of the countries in which they establish affiliates.

Part of the answer, it must be remarked, emerges tacitly from what has already been said: total inflows and outflows on direct investment account run at small percentages of the total balance of payments of the various countries; and the total balance of payments is itself a smallish aggregate in the total economy of the countries. Thus the total inflows and outflows on all balance of payments items for the United States in 1966, as shown in Appendix, Table 8, running as they were at between $45–48 billion, represented only 6 per cent of the United States GNP. Direct investment flows, as we see it from the table, were no more than 6–7 per cent of balance of payments flows, so that direct investment flows were a very small percentage indeed of United States GNP. Community direct investment flows ran between $1\frac{1}{2}$–3 per cent of balance of payments totals, and the latter were about 21 per cent of GNP. In the case of the UK, direct investment accounted for 4–7 per cent of the balance of payments total at some $25·5 billion, and the latter equalled almost exactly 25 per cent of GNP.[1]

However, although the above places the question in its essential perspective, it does not lessen the need to explore the implications for capital resources more thoroughly.

A second preliminary observation is necessary. This is that there are some conceptual incongruities in the preoccupations which have been expressed about the effect of direct investment on capital resources. Ill-consequences have been ascribed both to the outflow of capital and to the inflow of capital. It has been said that capital exports deprive a country of resources that would otherwise increase its own domestic assets, and all the profit, employment and general prosperity that go with this. On the other hand, it has been feared that capital imports lead to a draw–off of profits to foreign destinations, and to an increase of foreign-held

[1] Source of GNP figures: OECD *National Accounts of OECD Countries 1950–1968*.

assets. However, it follows that if capital exports deprive the donor nation of essential industrial and commercial activity and the return on these, then these advantages must go to the recipient nations. Similarly, if the recipient nations' payments of profits are bad for those nations, then they must be good for the donor nation to which they go. That such a contradiction of views about the same phenomenon should arise in direct flows between donor and recipient nations, i.e. between developed and developing countries, is perhaps understandable. It is less so when the same fears are expressed simultaneously in industrialised countries engaged in both the import and the export of capital. It is difficult to accept the proposition in those cases that the outflow of capital is bad for the nation's economy, and at the same time the inflow is bad for that economy. What is perhaps most surprising is that the principle normally held to apply to commercial transactions is not accepted here. It is commonly agreed that trade, in goods and services for instance, is beneficial both ways—that both imports and exports are desirable, and indeed essential to both parties. The international sale of a piece of merchandise, or a service, is a transaction from which both the buyer and the seller derive a benefit. Curiously, perhaps, this principle has not been applied to the transfer across borders of investment capital, which is equally a commercial transaction. It could well be, therefore, that the effect of investment capital movements is to benefit both parties to the operation.

However, this is an issue of general principle to which the present study has little relevance. What follows, therefore, will not enter into this particular debate. The present study, which is an empirical one, will merely measure the investment flows, on the one hand, and the national resources from which they are drawn, or to which they contribute, on the other, and compare the size of one with the other.

Some definitional points firstly arise. It can be said with some justice that the income inflows on capital exports are in fact a re-import of that capital, since they consist of profits and dividends which return to the cash flow of the parent company, and are, to a large extent, reconverted into long-term assets. Accordingly, it might be concluded that capital exports, net of income returns, only should be considered. However, for no reasons other than a desire for clarity, and for overstating rather than understating the capital flows involved, only gross capital exports will be considered for the moment. The question then arises whether the capital flows taken should include reinvested profits. It can be contended that since reinvested earnings obviate the need for fresh capital streams from the parent company, the resources of the home country are not drawn upon. On the other hand, it could be stated with equal cogency that had reinvested profits in fact been brought home by the parent company, they would have fallen into the reservoir of national assets in that country, and that in their absence, the latter suffers a real deprivation of resources. For the purposes of the present study, it has been decided to regard reinvested profits as capital outflows by the parent country.

However, when capital inflows into the host country are considered, a new factor comes into the calculation; this is that of the total cash flow of the subsidiaries in question. As has been said earlier, the act of outward investment is to create in the host country a unit of new business activity— the subsidiary of the capital exporting parent company. This subsidiary, in its ensuing life, does not act merely as a magnet for fresh capital inputs from the parent company. It engages in expanding business, which generates a new cash flow. This comprises the unremitted profits of the parent company, and sizeable provisions, before profit, for depreciation. These internal finances, going for the most part, as they do, into new long-term assets, necessarily create new capital. Although provisions for depreciation and the balance of unremitted profits are not an emanation from the parent company, it follows indubitably that if that company had not set up a subsidiary in the host country, a cash flow would not have arisen, and the new capital ensuing from this would not have materialised.

It is perhaps important to define the significance of the concept 'depreciation' in the present context. If the word is taken in its strict accountancy sense—that of financial provisions for the replacement of worn-out fixed assets—then it might be felt that funds set aside by international companies for the purpose of depreciation are not a contribution to the growth of capital in the host country. However, the word is used at this point in a somewhat fuller sense. Additions of wholly new capital are, in any country at any given time, very small in relation to the total stock of existing capital. If this existing capital stock were not continuously replenished, then the total capital assets of the country would fairly swiftly diminish. Provisions for depreciation are therefore, in an economic sense, a genuine contribution to capital. Another aspect of this matter must be considered. In a period of rapid technological innovation combined with economic growth, such as the present one, the replacement of one worn-out capital asset by another new, and identical one, is a largely inapplicable concept. Retiring assets are normally replaced by assets which are both technologically more advanced, and of larger capacity. The process of providing for depreciation is therefore indistinguishable from the act of financing new investment.

The use of the concept 'depreciation', referring as it does to funds generated by the activities of the international company inside the host country, may also, it may be felt, entail an overstatement of the contribution of international companies, since depreciation results from the productive efforts of the host country and its population. It might, however, be more misleading to conclude that depreciation funds are solely the product of the host country's efforts. The point in reality is a broader one, applying to the whole cash flow, including profits, of the subsidiary, and indeed to the benefits conferred on host countries, not only by direct investment as a whole, but by the process of international exchange as a whole. The contribution made by the host country element cannot, and should not, be disclaimed; nevertheless, the benefit claimed for direct investment is precisely that it harnesses the respective energies and advantages of the host element and the international company in a way which is beneficial to both, as was also shown in Chapter 1 above. The host country increases its own store of capital, whilst the country of the international company derives profits from the undertaking. As was earlier said, this is a point which is basic to international trans- actions as a whole. It could be demonstrated with equal facility that the sale of visible merchandise into one country by another is dependent on, and reinforces, the sales and merchanting potential of the recipient country, whilst giving profit to the country of origin. The point is one of broad economic and political philosophy, into which the present study cannot proceed further.

Of similar broad import worth treating in the present context is finally the view that direct investment by international companies is merely a substitute for domestic investment, and constitutes, therefore, in the final analysis, no genuine addition to the host country's capital. This point can be viewed in two ways: it may well be thought that the international company, having greater capital, technological and managerial resources, is able to open up opportunities which cannot be created by indigenous industry. On the other hand, it may be felt that in the absence of the com- petitive obstacle posed by the international company, the requisite resources would have become available to local industry. These hypotheses cannot be pursued further in the present context. The present study is an empirical observation of the course of historical events. What happened, in reality, was that the investments were in fact made by international companies, and the present study examines the financial results which ensued.

There is of course another element, not so far mentioned, making up the full cash flow of a non-wholly-owned subsidiary—the profit arisings due to the minority shareholder. It could be argued that these equity acquisitions, and the profits deriving from them, similarly would not have materialised without the presence of the parent as the main shareholder, and that these profit arisings obtained should be included in the contri- bution to the host country's capital resources. However, partly because of the historical origins of minority shareholdings in the case of many subsidiaries, and partly out of a desire for under- rather than overstate- ment of the foreign investor's contribution, this has not been included for present purposes. The total cash flow of subsidiaries, and the relative size of minority equity, will however be considered at an appropriate stage later in the study.

On the other hand, it may be felt that an analogous allocation of depreciation flows as between parent and subordinate equity holders should also be made. This has not been done, since the funds concerned are those set aside by the subsidiary, according to normal company practice, for its own continuance, and by definition, before a profit is struck for distribution to shareholders, whether these be the parent company or the local equity holders. The funds therefore appear to be a true contribution to the host nation's capital resources.

It may therefore with justice be said that the effect of inward investment on the capital resources of the host country derives not only from the flow of cross-frontier capital from the parent company, but also from total cash flow of the subsidiary companies, consisting both of the reinvested earnings of the parent, and the provisions for depreciation of the subsidiary.

For the purposes of analysis it will be best to split direct investment capital flows into its two obvious components: (a) Capital Outflows; (b) Capital Inflows.

(a) CAPITAL OUTFLOWS

As was apparent from Chapter 1, capital outflows are, for practical purposes, confined to the industrialised countries.

The size of these outflows has already been shown in Chapter 1. For the purposes of the aggregates which will now be considered, it is better to show these, not as a global total for the five-year period 1964–68, but as an annual average figure for that period, viz.:

Capital Outflows of Developed Countries 1964–68

	Annual Average
	$m.
US	4,813
UK	834
European Community	1,011
All Developed Countries	7,028

SOURCE: IMF. Cf. Chapter 1 above.

The reservoir from which this capital is drawn is in the first place the total capital resources of the nations concerned; i.e. all the capital which goes into the financing of industrial and commercial enterprise, public and private, in the countries concerned, into government expenditure on the nations' infrastructure and amenities to the population, and into the reserves of financial assets held by both the public and private sector; in other words, the total reservoir is that summed up in the figure for aggregate 'Gross addition to National Wealth'; i.e. the total of government, corporate and personal saving and depreciation of the countries concerned. This data is available in the OECD Accounts. The following is the relation of one to the other:

Annual Average 1964–68	*(1) Capital Outflows $m.*	*(2) Gross Addition to National Wealth $m.*	*(3) % (1) of (2)*
US	4,813	140,246	3·4
UK	834	19,454	4·3
European Community	1,011	83,774	1·2
All Developed Countries[2]	7,028	321,493	2·2

SOURCE: OECD *National Accounts of OECD Countries 1950–1968*, Part III, Table 10. (National currencies converted at 1964 exchange rate.)

However, although direct investment capital exports are undoubtedly a withdrawal from the total capital pool of the country concerned, it is worth considering what the size of this withdrawal is, in relation to capital specifically reserved for the formation of fixed assets. The major part of international companies' input of capital into their subsidiaries abroad is for the creation of plant, machinery and other fixed installations. The following is a comparison along these lines:

	(1) Capital Outflows $m.	*(2) Gross Domestic Fixed Asset Formation $m.*	*(3) % (1) of (2)*
US	4,813	127,690	3·8
UK	834	18,997	4·4
European Community	1,011	78,100	1·3
All Developed Countries[3]	7,028	299,300	2·3

The offtake shown by the above still appears to be small.

A final and closer comparison is now necessary. What is the relationship of direct investment outflows to fixed asset formation in those particular industries which provide the major direct investment flows abroad? These can best be collated from Table 4 ('Gross Domestic Fixed Asset Formation by Industry of Use') of the OECD's National Accounts 1950–68. The following industry sectors have been chosen (numbering follows that used in the OECD Table).

1. Agriculture, forestry and fishing.
2. Mining and quarrying.
3. Manufacturing and construction.

[2] All OECD countries included under this figure. This differs slightly from the IMF coverage in that Australia, New Zealand and Malta are excluded. The difference is, however, marginal.
[3] See Note to previous Table.

5. Transportation and communication.
8. Other service industries.

(1. above is included since this covers outward investment in plantations, timber, etc.) The following are the comparisons:

	(1) Capital Outflows $m.	(2) Fixed Asset Formation by Relevant Industries $m.	(3) % (1) of (2)
US	4,813	53,204	9·0
UK	834	11,127	7·5
European Community	1,011	45,646[4]	2·2
All Developed Countries	7,028	224,352[5]	3·1

The overall results of the above three comparisons therefore seem to show that by various standards of measurement, even those on a relatively narrow basis, the expatriation of capital through the agency of direct investment abroad does not appear likely to lead to a serious shortage of domestic resources.

A final observation, before leaving this aspect, is important. Industrialised countries, as has already been said, are the main source, but also the main destination, of direct investment capital. The impact of capital inflows on the aggregate finances of the host nation will of course be considered in the next Section, but it must meanwhile be noted that capital inflows offset capital outflows, and that the true loss of capital to a country conducting both inward and outward investment is the residual of these two.

This residual can be computed from the data already produced in Chapter 1 above, and is as follows:

Net Capital Outflows of Developed Countries 1964–68
Annual Average

	(1) Capital Outflows $m.	(2) Capital Inflows $m.	(3) Net Capital Outflows $m.
US	−4,813	+533	−4,280
UK	−834	+520	−314
European Community	−1,011	+1,713[6]	+702
All Developed Countries	−7,028	+5,245	−1,783

SOURCE: IMF.

[4] Includes gas, electricity and water in the case of Italy and the Netherlands.
[5] See Note[2] on previous page.
[6] Assuming that none of the $5,000 m. unrecorded reinvested profits (see Chapter 1, page 18) occurred in EEC countries. In fact it is likely that at least half of these were located in the Community; this would give a figure of some $2,213 m. annual average of capital inflows.

Some salient points emerge from the above table. The first is that the true capital loss for developed countries as a whole falls to just under $2,000 m., i.e. a third of the gross outflow, and that the European Community emerges as, in effect, a net gainer, rather than loser, of investment capital. When these net figures are compared with the national aggregates set out in the tables below, then the resulting percentages are seen to be very much smaller.

Net Capital Outflows of Developed Countries as a Proportion
of Gross Asset Formation, Gross Fixed Asset Formation and
Fixed Asset Formation in Relevant Industries
1964–68 Annual Average

Per cent	Gross Addition to National Wealth[7]	Gross Domestic Fixed Asset Formation	Fixed Asset Formation in Relevant Industries
US	3·1	3·4	8·0
UK	1·6	1·7	2·8
European Community[8]	0·8	0·9	1·5
All Developed Countries	0·4	0·6	0·8

Source of national accounts data:
OECD: *National Accounts of OECD Countries 1950–1968*, Country Tables 10.

The figures shown above can only reinforce the view that the effect of direct investment capital flows upon the major financial aggregates of developed countries are very small.

(*b*) CAPITAL INFLOWS

As already remarked, these must be taken to include (i) new capital input from the parent companies; (ii) reinvested earnings of the parent companies; (iii) provisions for depreciation of the subsidiary companies. The first two of these items of cash flow arise from data already compiled in Chapter 1, and are as follows:

	Annual Average 1964–68
Capital Inflows	*$b.*
into Developed Countries	5·25
Developing Countries	1·90

To the above should be added data for depreciation. This is available in the excellent series: 'Sources and Uses of Funds of Foreign Affiliates of US Firms' published by the United States Department of Commerce in the *Survey of Current Business*, and in the comprehensive data published by the British Department of Trade and Industry. Official data is not

[7] Net contribution to relevant aggregate in each case.
[8] Since the Community is a net recipient of capital, the percentages represent an *addition* to, rather than withdrawal from, the national aggregate.

published for international companies based in other countries, but aided by the advice kindly given by a large number of European companies,[9] an estimate can be made. Details of the calculations involved are shown in Table 13 in the Statistical Appendix.

As will be seen from the Appendix Table, total depreciation was as follows:

1964–68—Annual Average

	$b.
In Developed Countries	3·8
Developing Countries	2·2

Combining the two, total retained profits and depreciation was as follows:

1964–68—Annual Average

	$b.
In Developed Countries	9·1
Developing Countries	4·2

These figures can now be set against the overall financial data of the countries concerned. It is worth taking developed countries first:

(i) Capital Inflows into Developed Countries

A major point arises immediately. It will be seen from the above figures that although developed countries are net exporters of capital as such, the overall balance, taking into account the generation of new capital by foreign-owned subsidiaries in those countries, produces a net addition to their domestic capital stock; that is to say:

	$b.
Total withdrawals of capital in the form of outward investment:	7·0
Total generation of capital consequent upon inward investment:	9·1

This effect arises from the inherent nature of business—whether national or international—remarked upon earlier. Business undertakings, once established, rely heavily on internally-generated funds for the creation of new capital; thus an inflow of investment capital, where it is smaller than the concurrent outflow in the same country, will by nature of the internal financing propensity of the inward subsidiaries more than make up for the loss of domestic resources represented by the capital exports. The parallel effect as regards income on the export of capital has already been seen in Chapter 1. The same propensity to generate internal capital

[9] See reference on page 12.

provides not only a growing stock of assets in the country in which investment is made, but a high flow of profits, in relation to new capital input, to the country of the parent company. This phenomenon appears to confirm the suggestion made (see page 41 above) that both forms of capital investment—inward and outward—can be of benefit to the participant countries. Inward investment brings a complement to the capital resources of the domestic economy; outward investment brings a high return in relation to the capital employed.

This being said, it remains necessary to quantify the total contribution of capital through inward investment, by comparison with the overall financial aggregates of the host countries concerned. The following table, based on those produced in the foregoing, illustrates this for developed countries as a whole.

Capital Inflows into Developed Countries as
a Proportion of Major Financial Aggregates
1964–68 Annual Average

	(1) Capital Inflows $m.	(2) As percentage of Gross Domestic Fixed Asset Formation	(3) As percentage of Fixed Asset Formation by Relevant Industries
US[10]	762	0·6	1·4
UK[11]	1,060	5·5	9·5
European Community[12]	2,844	3·6	6·2
All Developed Countries	9,100	3·0	3·6

As will be seen from the percentages shown, the impact on the aggregate capital of the host country is in all cases less than a proportion of 10 per cent, and for the developed world as a whole, less than 4 per cent.

(ii) Conclusions on Capital Inflows into Developed Countries

It is now time to gather together all the aspects of capital inflows, and to attempt to sum them up as a single force. At this point it is relevant to bring in the element of income flows. This has been alluded to at various points above. It was noted that income can be regarded as a reconstitution

[10] Depreciation in US: Sources quoted for UK investment ($47·9 m.). Other countries assumed equivalent to ratio of assets to assets held by UK. (Average 1967–68: *Survey of Current Business*, October 1970, page 35, $150·9 m.; plus oil (estimated).)
[11] Depreciation in UK: *Board of Trade Journal* 26/1/68; *Business Monitor*, Series M4, 1971, Table 39. Accumulated Depreciation end 1965: £699·6 m.; end 1968: £1,187·9 m.; Annual Average provision: £162·7 m.; add oil £30 m. (estimated); total annual average $540 m.
[12] Depreciation in Community: Sum of UK and US affiliate provisions for depreciation. Sources as above. Other depreciation: assumed equivalent to ratio of US- and UK-held assets to total foreign assets in the Community in 1966.

of the capital exported by the investing country, and this must now be taken into account; also it has been seen that income returns tend over the course of time to grow larger than the new outward flows of capital. In short, we can now distinguish clearly the balance of payments effects of direct investment from that on domestic capital resources. Thus, for the balance of payments, the flows taken were:

> Capital outflows *less* reinvested earnings; *minus* capital inflows *less* reinvested earnings; *plus* income inflows *less* reinvested earnings; *minus* income outflows *less* reinvested earnings.

For the effect on domestic capital resources, the following, clearly, is the appropriate formula:

> Capital inflows (including reinvested earnings); plus depreciation on inward assets; *minus* capital outflows (including reinvested earnings); *plus* income inflows less reinvested earnings; *minus* income outflows *less* reinvested earnings.

The combined effect of these flows constitutes the net impact on the pool of domestic capital available in the country concerned. This figure can now be set out for developed countries as a whole, and for the US, the UK, and the Community.

Net Effect of Direct Investment on Domestic Capital Resources
1964–68 Annual Average[13]

$m.	Capital Inflow including Reinvested Earnings	Deprecia-tion	Capital Outflow including Reinvested Earnings	Income Inflow less Reinvested Earnings	Income Outflow less Reinvested Earnings	Net Balance
US	+533	+229	−4,813	+3,303	−330	−1,078
UK	+520	+540	−834	+758	−339	+645
Community	+1,713	+1,131	−1,011	+455	−422	+1,866
All Developed Countries	+5,245	+3,813	−7,028	+4,615	−2,468	+4,177

This, then, sets out the total effect of all of these ebbs and flows on the domestic capital pool of the countries concerned. It will be seen that the combined forces of two-way capital flows, high depreciation accumulations, and high income returns in relation to capital exports, lead to an overall positive balance.

It remains for this final balance to be compared with the global financial aggregates used above.

The following is the comparison:

---

[13] See also Appendix, Tables 5–12.

Direct Investment Balance in Developed Countries as a Proportion
of Main Financial Aggregates
1964–68 Annual Average

	(1) Net Direct Investment Capital Balance	(2) Gross Domestic Fixed Asset Formation	(3) (1) as % of (2)	(4) Fixed Asset Formation in Relevant Industries	(5) (1) as % of (4)
$m.					
US	−1,078	127,690	−0·8	53,204	−2·0
UK	645	18,997	3·4	11,127	8·4
Community	1,866	78,100	2·3	45,646	4·1
All Developed Countries	3,962	299,300	1·3	224,352	1·8

Once again, compared with the great magnitudes of the economy at large, direct investment flows are seen to be small.

(iii) Capital Inflows into Developing Countries

In the case of developing countries, the conceptual position is much simpler, since the capital movements are in one direction only, i.e. inwards.[14] As has been seen, these inflows averaged, in the period 1964–68:

> $2·0 billion including reinvested earnings.
> To this must be added the figure for depreciation of $1·8 billion; making a total capital accretion annually in developing countries of $3·8 billion.

An important point can be immediately discerned. The size of depreciation provisions is virtually equal to the parents' capital input, and thus doubles the capital contribution apparent from the balance of payments account alone. Indeed, although as has already been shown, the immediate balance of payments effect of direct investment flows on developing countries may be felt to be adverse, the total effect on the capital resources of developing countries is very different. Total capital accretions now outweigh the investment income payments of $2·7 billion annually that have to be made, and the overall effect on the capital resources balance of the developing countries is favourable. If a global capital balance, as set out above for the developed countries, is now constructed for developing countries, this emerges most clearly.

In this case, the formula to be followed, of course, is:

> Capital imports, including reinvested earnings; *plus* depreciation; *minus* investment income outflows, *less* reinvested earnings.

The figures under this formula are as follows:

[14] But see footnote [15] (opposite.)

Direct Investment Capital Balance of Developing Countries
1964–68 Annual Average

$ b. Capital Imports +1·5	Reinvested Earnings +0·5	Depreciation +1·8	Income Outflows less Reinvested Earnings −2·4	Net Balance +1·4

The net contribution to capital resources shown by the table furnishes further evidence in support of the notion put forward earlier that direct investment, being a commercial transaction, should be of advantage to both parties; and that immediate balance of payments appearances should not divert attention from these benefits.

The data published by the OECD on the 'National Accounts of Less Developed Countries' permits the assembly of representative figures for gross domestic product and for gross fixed capital formation. This figure has certain limitations, in that it relates only to a limited number of major countries in the developing world,[15] and that in certain cases it does not distinguish between public and private fixed capital formation—although the indications are that the latter forms the major part of the total. However, the figures derived by this means no doubt constitute a sound indication of the probable total for the developing world as a whole. This data shows a total value for gross domestic product, as an annual average for the years 1963–68, of $187 billion, and an annual average value of $29·26 billion for gross fixed capital formation. The net capital contribution to developing countries thus appears to equal about 1 per cent of gross domestic product, and about 5 per cent of total fixed capital formation.

Data on smaller financial aggregates—particularly fixed asset formation in specific industries—is not available. However, there is some scope for further analysis on the basis of regions. For Latin America, a succinct compilation of data on gross investment (i.e. gross fixed investment and changes in stocks) has recently been published by the Inter-American Development Bank.[16] According to this analysis, total gross investment at current prices in six major Latin American countries—Argentina, Brazil, Colombia, Mexico, Peru and Venezuela—ran at an annual average of £28,755 m. in the years 1964–68. The authors of the study state that this amount was equivalent to some 86·6 per cent of total investment in Latin America as a whole during this period. Thus it can be assumed that total

[15] Following are the countries in question: Argentina, Brazil, Chile, Colombia, Mexico, Peru, Venezuela, Ceylon, China (Taiwan), South Korea, Thailand, Kenya, Pakistan, the Philippines, Morocco, Nigeria, Tunisia and India.
N.B. The figures include public capital formation in all Latin American countries, and in Pakistan, the Philippines, Morocco, Nigeria, Tunisia and India (1959–63).
[16] Antonin Basch and Milic Kybal: *Capital Markets in Latin America*, published for the Inter-American Development Bank, Praeger, 1970.

gross investment in Latin America in the quinquennial under consideration was some $33,200 m.

A table can now be constructed for total capital input into Latin
America. This will show, first: the gross contribution, i.e. capital imports including reinvested earnings, plus depreciation; and then the net
contribution to the domestic capital stock, i.e. capital imports including
reinvested earnings, plus depreciation, less investment income payments,
excluding reinvested earnings.

Gross and Net Capital Input into Latin America
1964–68 Annual Average

	$m.
Capital Input including Reinvested Earnings	903[17]
Depreciation	1,271[18]
Total Gross Capital Input	1,670
Percentage of Gross Asset Formation	5·0%
Income Outflow less Reinvested Earnings	1,230[19]
Net Capital Input	440
Percentage of Gross Asset Formation	1·3%

The above table confirms the general conclusions which have so far
emerged in the present study. When all flows have been taken into account,
Latin America derived an absolute addition to capital resources from
inward direct investment. On the other hand, the overall financial aggregates of the Continent are very large in relation to this inflow. This
again has an historical precedent suggesting that the small relative size of
the capital input does not necessarily detract from its significance.[20]

[17] Cf. Appendix, Table 2.
[18] Cf. Appendix, Table 13.
[19] Cf. Appendix, Table 3.
[20] 'Between 1869 and 1878, net foreign investment in the US accounted for 10·7 per cent
of domestic net capital formation, 6·2 per cent of domestic gross capital formation and
1·3 per cent of gross national product. The percentages for the following decade were
3·0 per cent, 1·8 per cent and 0·4 per cent. In the ten years 1889–98, however, there was a
net capital outflow of 1·1 per cent, 0·6 per cent and 0·1 per cent....' John H. Dunning:
Studies in International Investment page 171. George Allen & Unwin Ltd., London, 1970.

CHAPTER 3

Effect on Financial Markets

So far, the analysis has dealt with the internal financing of international companies; that is to say, with the input of fresh capital and reinvested earnings by the parent company, the accumulation of depreciation, and the repayment of income by the subsidiary to the parent company; and it has considered the net contribution of these flows to the capital resources of the countries of both the parent and the subsidiary.

It is now time to consider the external financing of the international companies. This will permit the measurement of the remaining ways in which international companies affect the economies in which they operate. These include the draw upon fresh capital through minority equity recruitment; the recourse to long- and short-term borrowing in the local capital and money markets, and the reallocation of capital through the distribution of dividends to minority shareholders.

It is evident that the analysis will not need to examine the external financing of the parent company itself. Insofar as locally recruited capital by the parent is used for commercial activities inside the parent's country, that company is acting as a domestic company, and its affairs do not come within the purview of the present study. Capital recruited from abroad, and used in the country of the parent company, falls into the same category. Capital sent by the parent company, whether obtained locally or from abroad, to other countries, constitutes a deduction from the capital resources of the parent company's country, and this has been measured in the relevant section above. Similarly, capital accruing to the parent company in the form of income returned by subsidiaries abroad has been measured as a net contribution to the parent country's capital resources. The present section of the study will therefore deal only with the external financing of the foreign subsidiaries of international companies. A useful introduction to this point can be made in the form of some flow of funds tables. The following illustrate the flows of funds in United States subsidiaries in developed and in developing countries.

The following two tables present a picture of the whole financing of American subsidiaries; that is to say, not simply the fund flows with the

Sources and Uses of Funds of US Affiliates in Developed Countries
(Mining and smelting, petroleum and manufacturing industries)
Average 1964, 1965, 1967, 1968

%	Sources	$m.	Uses	$m.	%
100					100
	OTHER	177	PROFITS	947	
97			AND		
	FUNDS	974	DIVIDENDS		
	FROM				
	US				85
			OTHER ASSETS	657	
82					
	FUNDS	1,597			75
	OBTAINED				
	ABROAD		CURRENT ASSETS	1,093	
			(Inventories		
			$426 m.)		
			(Current Re-		
			ceivables		
			$667 m.)		57
56			FIXED ASSETS	3,603	
	CASH FLOW	3,554	(Property,		
	(Net earnings after		Plant &		
	tax, $1,638)		Machinery)		
30					
	(Depreciation				
	$1,916 m.)				
0					0
Total		6,302		6,302	

SOURCE: 'Sources and Uses of Funds of US Owned Foreign Affiliates', *Survey of Current Business*, November 1970, 'Canada' and 'Europe'.

parent, but also funds obtained from sources other than the parent, and income paid to recipients other than the parent. The predominance of the role of cash flow on the one hand (55–60 per cent of total sources), and of expenditure on fixed assets (50–60 per cent) in the uses of funds, is evident.

Owing to the nature of flow of funds tabulations and to the coverage of companies in this data collection, an exact parallel cannot be drawn

Sources and Uses of Funds of us Affiliates in Developing Countries
(*Mining and smelting, petroleum and manufacturing industries*)
Average 1964, 1965, 1967, 1968

%	Sources	$m.	Uses	$m.	%
100					100
98	OTHER	113	PROFITS	1,231	
	FUNDS FROM US	699	AND DIVIDENDS		
84					
	FUNDS OBTAINED ABROAD	1,171			75
			OTHER ASSETS	494	
					65
			CURRENT ASSETS (Inventories $374 m.)	828	
60					
	CASH FLOW (Net earnings after tax, $1,711)	2,920	(Current Receivables $454 m.)		
					48
			FIXED ASSETS (Property, Plant & Machinery)	2,387	
25					
	(Depreciation $1,209 m.)				
0					0
Total		4,903		4,979	

SOURCE: 'Sources and Uses of Funds of us Owned Foreign Affiliates', *Survey of Current Business*, November 1970, 'Latin American Republics & Other Western Hemisphere' and 'Other Areas'.

with the data—mainly of balance of payments origin—used in the foregoing chapters. In the first place, as will be seen from the table headings, the coverage of industries is restricted to those engaged in manufacturing, petroleum, and mining and smelting only. Other forms of direct investment, particularly in transport, services, finance and marketing, are not included. As has earlier been pointed out, inclusion of these industries should lead to a relatively small uprating of the figure for depreciation and fixed assets. A larger uprating would be required for cash flow, funds from the US, and profit and dividend payments. As against this, inclusion of financial undertakings, given their specialised nature, would involve a disproportionate, and for present purposes not highly meaningful, enlargement of the figures for funds obtained abroad and current and other assets; given the nature of banking business, these items would in any case be largely self-cancelling. Moreover, the purpose of the above flow of funds tables is to illustrate the relative weighting of items on both sides of the balance in the case of multinational corporations, and the latter are not concentrated in the transport, services, finance and marketing industries. It has not been thought necessary, therefore, to gross up this particular set of data. Nevertheless, the point will be reverted to at a relevant stage later in the study.[1]

The centre of attention in the flow of funds tables, for present purposes, is the item entitled 'Funds obtained Abroad'. This consists of the subsidiary's borrowing from local sources, and its acquisition of capital through local equity issues; also its borrowing from other affiliates of the group from third countries, and its trade credit locally and with third countries. As will be seen, although the item as a whole accounts for about 26 per cent of the total sources of funds, only a part relates to borrowing in the capital and money markets of the host country. The remainder of this section of the study will be devoted to an analysis of these components. It is worth remarking at the outset, however, that the local equity acquisitions are extremely small (about 1·5 per cent of total sources in developed countries, and about 2 per cent in the case of developing countries). This means that total cash flow, and the distribution of profits and dividends shown, also relate almost entirely to movements between the subsidiary and the parent. It follows from this that the item 'Funds from US' underestimates the total input of capital from the parent, since the latter's participation in retained income (included in 'Cash Flow') is virtually 100 per cent. It follows that the parent's input of capital (includ-

---

[1] Other differences are that interest payments are not included in the income distribution (profits and dividends) shown in the Sources and Uses table, whereas it is included in the income payments shown in the general data; however, interest payments are very small (less than $½ m. in 1969). Total profits of branches are included in income payments in the foregoing sections, whereas only those actually remitted are included in 'profits and dividends' in the flow of funds tables. This does not basically affect the comparisons made in the earlier sections, as remarked therein. Flows of funds simply reflect more accurately the division between profits retained and remitted. However, it is likely that the use of branches rather than subsidiaries is more widespread amongst the industries omitted than those covered in the tables; i.e. among non–'multinational' companies. 'Funds from US' includes not only capital flows from the parents, but also funds supplied by direct shareholders in the United States and by banks and US commercial suppliers. On the other hand, payments made by the parent company for the acquisition of minority interests are excluded, since they go to stockholders outside the subsidiary.

ing depreciation), amounted to some 75 per cent of total resources in both developed and developing countries, largely exceeding the amounts devoted to the formation of fixed assets. This accords of course with the broad conclusions arrived at earlier.

Meanwhile, however, it is worth looking at some other flow of funds tabulations.

The British Board of Trade (now the Department of Trade and Industry) has provided, in its excellent triennial analysis (Overseas Investment Enquiry), total balance sheet items for British-owned foreign affiliates, for end-1965 and end-1968, which permit of conversion into a fund-flow table for the average of the three years in question. The only item missing from this compilation is the figure for the affiliates' total profit after tax, and their total payment of dividends and profits. The Reddaway Report on the 'Effects of UK Direct Investment Overseas' however showed the participation by the UK parent in the affiliates' total profits, and also the proportion of dividends and profits paid to the UK parent (actual earnings and dividends of the parent are included in the Department of Trade and Industry data). Use of the Reddaway ratio therefore permits the addition of the item missing from DTI's material. A caveat to be attached to this link is that the Reddaway material shows an average for the decade 1955–64, and itself relates to a group of companies constituting somewhat less than 50 per cent of the UK universe of companies which is covered by the DTI enquiry (49·9 per cent of total coverage in the case of developed countries; 36·2 per cent in the case of developing countries). However, the result, although approximate, seems reliable enough for the orders of magnitude required for the fund flow tables in question.[2]

The calculations provide the tables shown on pages 58 and 59 for the flow of funds of UK-owned affiliates in developed and in developing countries.

The limitations of the tables must not be overlooked. The magnitudes in themselves are necessarily of a high degree of approximation. Similarly entries merely for 'current liabilities', 'long-term liabilities', and 'current assets' are not in themselves statements of the borrowings, long- or short-term, of the affiliates. None the less, 'long-term liabilities' will be a close approximation to fixed interest borrowing. The figures do of course exclude balances with the parent company itself, and are therefore true measures, if perhaps exaggerated, of local funding by the subsidiaries. However, the tables appear none the less useful for their main purpose: that of an illustration of the financial structure of British over-

[2] In order to show the profit ratio separately for developed and developing countries, use has been made of further material, likewise sub-dividing the Reddaway data, which has been very kindly provided by the Department of Applied Economics at Cambridge University for the present study. This, of course, further reduces the relationship of the Reddaway sample to the universe of UK companies (down to about 40 per cent and 30 per cent respectively).

seas companies, both in themselves and in relation to the financing of American affiliates.

In both sets of tables, the high degree of self-financing through cash

Sources and Uses of Funds of UK Affiliates in Developed Countries
1964–68—Annual Average

%	Sources	$m.	Uses	$m.	%
100					100
	OTHER SOURCES	388·8	PROFITS AND DIVIDENDS	424·1	
85					
	CURRENT LIABILITIES	490·3			84
			CURRENT ASSETS	1,080·8	
67					
	LONG-TERM LIABILITIES	223·2			
59					
	FUNDS FROM PARENT	129·1			
54					
	CASH FLOW Profits after tax, $1,016·4 m.	1,469·4			
					44
			EXPENDITURE ON FIXED ASSETS	1,195·9	
17					
	(Depreciation $453·0 m.)				
0					0
Total		2,700·8		2,700·8	

flow mentioned earlier in the present study, can be discerned. Similarly, the low input of fresh capital from the parent (the item in the US tables 'Funds from the US' includes US bank loans and private investment, in addition to capital flows from the parent company) emerges clearly. Self-financing is seen to be larger in the case of developing countries than developed countries, and as a corollary to this, local borrowing also appears smaller. The higher cash flow figure, of course, reflects a higher ploughing-back of profits by the parent company. The lower figure for expenditure on fixed assets may well reflect the comparative concentration

Sources and Uses of Funds of UK Affiliates in Developing Countries
1964–68—Annual Average

%	Sources	$m.	Uses	$m.	%
100					100
	CURRENT LIABILITIES	200·8	OTHER USES (Provision for taxation, etc.)	9·1	
					99
81			DIVIDENDS AND	393·8	
	LONG-TERM LIABILITIES	20·7	PROFITS		
79					
	FUNDS FROM PARENT	25·2			
77					
	CASH FLOW Profits after tax, $674·8 m.	812·3			
					62
			CURRENT ASSETS	319·5	
					32
			EXPENDITURE ON FIXED ASSETS	336·6	
19					
	(Depreciation $207·8 m.)				
0					0
Total		1,059·0		1,059·0	

of manufacturing investment in developed, rather than in developing, countries.

The tables for US- and UK-based companies exhaust the sources of official data on flows of funds. A large number of international companies remain, largely in continental Europe, and considerable data has been collected from many of these for the purposes of the present study. Owing to inivitable variations in the nature of the data kindly provided, and to the fact that flow of funds analysis is not a uniform practice, it is not feasible to set out the data in precise tabular form. However, the results supplied suggest that European international companies' affiliates operate on much the same financial structure as those of United States and British parents, with perhaps—owing to the shorter maturity of most European investment—higher proportions for parents' financing, and lower ratios for dividend and profit payout to the parent. In the case of American and British companies, the slightly higher profit and dividend payout ratios shown for developing countries partly illustrate the higher degree of minority shareholding in those areas.

The subject of flow of funds and affiliates cannot be left without a reference to the invaluable work of Professor H. Lee Remmers—one of the few empirical analyses of the data available, outside official sources.[3] Professor Remmers' work presents an analysis on a flow basis of the balance sheets of 115 subsidiaries of foreign companies operating in the United Kingdom in the period 1960–67. Of these subsidiaries, 90 were American-owned, and 25 were European-owned. The study was confined to subsidiaries in manufacturing industry only, but this detracts little or nothing from its value. The results are shown in the table on page 61.

Professor Lee Remmers supplemented his analysis with a tabulation of the flow of funds in equivalent British companies. This has been included in the table as Column 4.

The table provides some useful evidence. In the first place, it brings out strikingly the lower level of self-financing by the subsidiaries of European companies, and the high reliance on parent companies' loan or share capital. The contrast in these items with United States and United Kingdom subsidiaries appears to bear out the possibility, mentioned earlier, that investment by European companies, being of younger maturity, has not so far attained its maximum profitability. This is reinforced by the high relative level of expenditure on fixed assets, and the lower payout of dividends shown on the 'Uses' side of the table. The interest of the comparison with British companies lies in the close similarity, in all flow items, with the average of foreign subsidiaries in the UK. This is perhaps a natural outcome. Domestic British companies will vary in age of establishment in the same way as foreign subsidiaries established in the UK, and since they are subject to the same economic conditions, their results will tend to be the same. Certainly the table casts doubt on the view that foreign-owned companies operating in a particular country are able to order their finances in a substantially different way to that of local industry. This point is particularly true as regards the payment of dividends (see Columns 3 and 4 of 'Uses').

[3] *The Strategy of Multinational Enterprise*: Michael Z. Brook and H. Lee Remmers; Longman 1970.

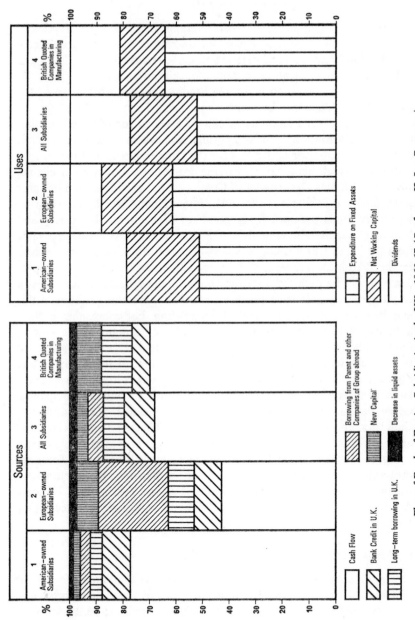

Flow of Funds of Foreign Subsidiaries in the UK—1960-67 (Professor H. Lee Remmers)

(a) Resort to Local Capital and Money Markets

The foregoing diagrammatic representations must now be translated, as far as possible, into hard figures for the impact of international companies' subsidiaries on local capital and money markets.

Two statistical elements are required for this purpose. Firstly, the actual sums of money comprised under the headings 'Funds from Abroad' for US companies; 'Current Liabilities' and 'Long-Term Liabilities' for UK companies, and such amounts as can be assessed for other companies, these broken down by separate regions and where possible countries; and the aggregates for all lending for the same countries and regions.

For the first element, data of varying degrees of accuracy are available. The United States Department of Commerce has produced an admirable series further breaking down the item 'Funds from Abroad', and showing separately funds obtained from long-term fixed interest borrowing and from bank credit. The same degree of accuracy is clearly not obtainable from the items 'Current Liabilities' and 'Long-Term Liabilities' produced by the British Department of Trade and Industry. For the sake of prudence it will be assumed that the whole of these items represent bank credit and long-term fixed interest borrowing respectively, although this may be a sizeable overstatement of the position. For companies of other nationalities it will be assumed, particularly in the light of the flow of funds table produced for the UK above, that the divergence from US and UK financial structures lies in the level of cash flow, dividend payout and capitalisation from the parent, and not in local borrowing; a figure for the latter can therefore be assessed pro rata to the US and UK companies. Given the varying degree of accuracy already stated, the analysis will show first the relationship of US affiliates' financing to the total local aggregates; then that of companies of all national origins as an aggregate.

Figures for the national financing aggregates will be drawn from appropriate sources such as the *OECD Financial Statistics*; the International Financial Service of the IMF; the United Nations Yearbook of National Accounts Statistics, and the OECD 'National Accounts of Developing Countries'.

(b) Local Borrowing of United States Affiliates

One preliminary point has to be stressed: neither the American nor the British data explicitly separates funds obtained by the affiliate in the host country from those obtained by the affiliates elsewhere; i.e. they do not eliminate borrowing in countries which are neither the country of the parent nor the country of the affiliates. However, the United States breakdown does permit of the elimination of 'Funds from foreign affiliates' which would comprise borrowings from other members of the group, and in particular from financial subsidiaries of the parent established in other countries. In theory, therefore, the residual figures which have to be used could comprise direct international borrowing in Eurodollars or Eurobonds, or in third country currencies, by the affiliates. However, since this is normally the work of the parent, or the financial subsidiaries of the group, the sums involved will be small, if not non-existent. The element both of international and of third country borrowing cannot be excluded from the UK figures, but as stated above, the error will be on the right side, since the effect will be to overstate rather than understate the recourse of British subsidiaries to local capital markets.

A remaining factor to be taken into account with respect to American companies is, as stated earlier, that the flow of funds data applies only to the mining, smelting, manufacturing and petroleum industries. These account for 78 per cent of all the United States foreign-held assets. The remaining 22 per cent consists of transport, service and trading establishments (approximately 12 per cent), and 'other', mainly banking and insurance (10 per cent). For the reasons earlier explained, relating to the self-cancelling nature of banking affiliates' claims and liabilities, and in order to exclude as far as possible Eurodollar, Eurobond, and other international borrowings, it seems desirable that 'other industries' should remain outside the categories under consideration. Transport, service and trading industries' local borrowing propensities do not appear to diverge widely from the average. Accordingly, the figures available from the US Department of Commerce flow of funds tables will be grossed up by 15·5 per cent.

A final point for consideration is that the United States figures in fact give a breakdown as between long- and short-term borrowings for the years 1965, 1967 and 1968 only. The figures presented will therefore be the average of these three years.

Local Borrowing of US Affiliates
Annual Average—1965, 1967, 1968

In	Long-Term $m.	Short-Term $m.
Developed Countries	425[4]	224
of which		
Canada	135	46
European Economic Community	159	154
Rest of Western Europe	100	37
Australia & New Zealand	32	−13
Developing Countries[5]	177	239
of which		
Latin America	27	122

[4] Individual items do not add to total owing to rounding.
[5] *Survey of Current Business*, November 1970, page 18, Table 3. 'All areas' less borrowing in developed countries as above.

Next, it is necessary to compare these borrowing figures with the total long- and short-term capital market of the countries in which US affiliates are shown to be operating, which is done in the following two tables:

Long-Term Fixed Interest Capital Markets
Annual Average—1964–68

		Total[6] $m.	Non-Financial Companies only $m.
Developed Countries			
Canada		1,626	466·8
EEC		12,180[7]	2,225·9
Other Western Europe		5,844	1,726·7
Australia ⎫ New Zealand ⎬		6,865[8]	217·0
	Total	26,515	4,636·4
Developing Countries			
Latin America		(2,000)[9]	

The above table shows first of all the long-term capital market (net new issues of bonds) for all purposes, and secondly the long-term borrowing of non-financial companies in each area. The figures are based on the *OECD Financial Statistics* for all countries except Australia, New Zealand and Latin America, where sources are shown. In the case of Latin America, no reliable statistics of securities issued are available, and

Bank Advances to the Private Sector
Annual Average—1964–68

	$000m.
Developed Countries	48·5
of which	
Canada	1·4
EEC	16·3
Other Europe	7·8
Australia & New Zealand	1·0
Developing Countries	
Latin America	1·9

SOURCE: IMF International Financial Statistics, August 1971—Country Tables line 32c (year to year increase).

[6] Public and Private Sector issues. Does not include straight loans to companies.
[7] *Total—OECD Financial Statistics*, II, 1970, Table III A.I.I. *Non-Financial Companies—OECD Financial Statistics*, II, 1970, Country Tables.
[8] SOURCE: *Public Sector—Reserve Bank of Australia Statistical Bulletin. Private Sector—Monthly Review of Business Statistics,* September 1971; N.Z.:n.a.
[9] Basch & Kybal *Capital Markets in Latin America* suggest total savings in financial institutions 1963 of $5,600 m. Assume 30 per cent of this placed to long-term loans.

the $2,000 m. shown above in brackets is only an approximate estimate derived from Basch & Kybal's *Capital Markets in Latin America*, prepared for the Inter-American Development Bank. As will be seen, compared either with total security issues, or with securities issued by companies only, the borrowing requirements of American affiliates are very small.

Again, United States affiliates' borrowings from banks appear to be very small indeed compared with the total advances available (it should be noted that the table at the foot of page 64 is in $000m., whereas the figures for American borrowing are in $m. The bank advances shown for the various countries is of course the total granted to the whole private sector, that is to say, to companies and to individuals alike. Sub-division of this total into bank advances to the company sector only is not possible on an up-to-date basis for the Community. However, the Segré Report[10] indicated that bank advances to companies in the Community in the years 1960–64 averaged $1,067 m. In the United Kingdom, total bank advances to non-financial companies averaged $789 m. in the years 1964–68.[11]

It is now time to add the British to the American totals of long- and short-term borrowing by affiliates.

Long- and Short-Term Borrowing
by US and UK[12] Affiliates
Annual Average—1964–68

In	Long-Term $m.	Short-Term $m.
Developed Countries	649	710
of which		
USA	58	64
Canada	144	115
EEC	226	272
Other Europe	83	87
Australia & New Zealand	122	119
Developing Countries	198	437
of which		
Latin America	27	158

It should be borne in mind, as stated earlier, that the UK figure added in is almost certainly an overestimate, comprising as it does total short- and long-term liabilities, and not simply borrowings from the capital and money market, and incorporating also borrowings outside the host country, including those in Eurodollar and Eurobond forms.

[10] Segre Report: page 352, Table 10—*Short Term Loans from Credit Institutions.*
[11] SOURCE: *Financial Statistics*, HMSO.
[12] SOURCE: UK figures *BoT Jnl.* 26/1/68, Tables 5 and 6. *Business Monitor M4*, 1971, Tables 35 and 36. Average is for end 1965 to end 1968.

It will be seen, however, that the combined totals still do not amount to a sizeable proportion of the total long- and short-term capital market in the various countries. As non-American-owned affiliates have now been included in the analysis, the United States itself has been introduced as a host country, and aggregate figures for the capital markets of the United States must now be compared. These are:

Capital Markets in the US
Annual Average 1964–68

	Long-Term[13]	Short-Term[14]
Total Issues *$000m.*	*Issues by Non-Financial Companies* *$000m.*	*Bank Advances* *$000m.*
25·7	9·4	22·5

Again, it will be seen that the ratio of foreign affiliates' borrowing to the total domestic capital market is very small.

It is now time to consider the total borrowing in the various countries of all international companies, that is to say, companies based not merely in the US and the UK, but in all other industrialised countries, including, principally, Western Europe. Since figures for borrowing by the latter companies are not available in any published and standardised form, it is not possible to suggest precise amounts, as has been done in the case of the US and the UK. However, an approximate notion of the weight of this borrowing can be obtained by assuming that the borrowing practices of these companies is akin to that of the US and the UK; in other words, that the increase in total funds obtained will be pro rata to the increase in net assets contributed by these companies, viz.:

Total Direct Investment Assets
1966

Host Country Country of Origin	Developed Countries $m.	%	Developing Countries $m.	%
US	36,662	60·0	18,137	63·7
UK	12,019	19·7	5,579	19·6
Others	12,436	20·3	4,750	16·7
Total	61,116	100·0	28,467	100·0

SOURCE: See Table 1—Statistical Appendix.

[13] SOURCE: *OECD Financial Statistics*, II, 1970, Total Issues Table III A.I.I. Issues by Non-Financial Companies Country Tables.
[14] SOURCE: IMF International Financial Statistics Country Tables line 32c (year to year increase).

Thus, US and UK direct investment assets in developed and developing countries respectively appear to amount to 79·7 per cent and 83·3 per cent of the total.

Total borrowing by international companies, this suggests, would be of the following order:

Total Borrowing by Affiliates of International Companies Annual Average—1964–68

In	Long-Term $m.	Short-Term $m.
Developed Countries	814	891
Developing Countries	237	524

In view of the limitations of accuracy of this method, it would be unwise to attempt an estimate by individual countries. However, it appears that aggregate long-term borrowing is some 6 per cent of total non-financial corporate issues in developed countries, whilst short-term borrowing is about 1¼ per cent of total bank advances.

Apart from borrowing, affiliates of international companies acquire new capital through the issue of shares in the host country. Here, only the US Department of Commerce provides viable figures. These show the following:

Local Equity Issues by Affiliates of US Companies Annual Average—1964–68

Developed Countries	$m.
Canada	42
EEC	50
Other Western Europe	37
Developing Countries	
Latin America	42

SOURCE: *Survey of Current Business*, November 1970, page 18, Table 3 (together with further information supplied separately by US Department of Commerce).

These issues can be compared with total equity issues in the various markets concerned, viz.:

Total Equity Issues

	$m.
Canada	547
EEC	2,686
Other Western Europe	2,210

SOURCE: *OECD Financial Statistics*, II, 1970.

As earlier stated, no official figures are supplied for UK and other countries, and an estimate cannot safely be made.

To complete this section, further reference should be made to Professor Lee Remmers' analysis of the operations of international company subsidiaries in the United Kingdom. As was shown on page 61, Professor Remmers' analysis established typical ratios for the sources of funds of these subsidiaries, of which those for 'bank credit' and 'long-term debt' were as follows:

Item	% of Total Sources of Funds
Bank Credit	9·9
Long-Term Debt	6·4

Professor Lee Remmers also showed that the payout of dividends equalled 22·4 per cent of the total fund flow.

The sample of companies taken by Professor Lee Remmers comprised companies in the manufacturing sector alone, excluding services, banking insurance and oil.

United Kingdom balance of payments statistics give total dividend outflows from foreign subsidiaries in manufacturing and service industries, including distribution, but excluding banking, insurance, and oil. If it is assumed, as is admissible, that fund flows concentrate heavily on manufacturing activities, and that moreover the borrowing practices of service and distribution industries is akin to that of manufacturing industries, then it is permissible, given these data, to gross up the Lee Remmers results to obtain a total fund flow for all foreign subsidiaries in manufacturing services and distribution in the UK.

The dividend payout of these industries averaged, according to UK Balance of Payments statistics, $250 m., period 1964–68. Given that this is equivalent to 22·4 per cent of the total financing flows of all subsidiaries, then the latter was:

$1,116 m. annually.

As is known, bank credit and long-term debt were equal to 9·9 per cent and 6·4 per cent of the above figure.

Thus, on the Lee Remmers basis, total borrowings by foreign subsidiaries in the UK in the period would appear to be

Item	$m.
Bank Credit	111
Long-Term Debt	71·4

This can now be compared with the total bank borrowing and long-term borrowing of all British companies in manufacturing and distribution over the period.[15]

[15] SOURCE: *Business Monitor M3*, 1971.

Item	$m. Foreign Subsidiaries	$m. British Companies	% Foreign Subsidiaries of Total Borrowing
Bank Credit	111	493	18·4
Long-Term Debt	71·4	854	7·8

(c) Expenditure on Fixed Assets

The present study is concerned with the purely financial role of international corporations. To speak, therefore, of the specific conversion of these financial assets into physical assets is to go outside the strict confines of the subject. On the other hand, the creation and maintenance of physical assets is an outward and visible sign of the contribution of international investment to the resources of the countries concerned; and a significant element of the funds assembled in the various ways depicted in the foregoing—through direct capital flows, provisions for depreciation, retained earnings, and external financing—goes into these concrete forms. It may therefore be of interest at this stage to attempt briefly to assess the level of expenditure on fixed assets by companies engaged in direct investment abroad, and the relationship of this expenditure to total activity in the host countries.

Table 14 in the Statistical Appendix enumerates this expenditure within the limits of accuracy permitted by existing data. As will be seen, there is firm data available for expenditures by United States and United Kingdom-based companies, whilst expenditure by the remainder can be estimated with reasonable reliability.

It will be seen that total expenditure on fixed assets by all companies in all countries amounted, in the period 1964–68, on an annual average basis, to some $10,814 m. Of this, $4,026 m. was spent in developing countries, and $6,788 m. was spent in developed countries.

A total for fixed asset formation in relevant industries was shown for developed countries on page 45. As will be seen, this activity was valued at some $224,352 m. at an annual average over the period. Expenditure on fixed assets by international companies was thus equal to 2·7 per cent of this. This figure, again, appears to reflect the fact that operations by international companies, although large by industrial standards, still rank fairly small in the very great magnitudes of the economies in which they operate.

For developing countries, a figure for gross fixed capital formation of $29,266 m. for the annual average of the period 1964–68 was quoted on page 51. Against this, the total expenditure on fixed assets by international companies of some $4,026 m. represents a percentage of 14 per cent.

Again, therefore, the general conclusion reached hitherto, i.e. that even in developing countries the share of international companies' activities in overall economic aggregates is fairly small, appears to be borne out.

There are no doubt exceptions to the above rule. Figures have in fact been calculated for the UK which suggest that that country shows ratios somewhat higher. Professor Lee Remmers' compilation shows that companies in his sample spent £822·6 m. on fixed assets in the period 1960–67 (aggregate for the period). This sample comprised a selection only of companies in manufacturing industry. Board of Trade data shows that all foreign companies engaged in manufacturing on the UK had at end-1967 assets of £2,046 m., as against the total of £1,797 m. quoted by Professor Lee Remmers for his own sample. Adjusting the data by this ratio, total expenditure on fixed assets by foreign companies in manufacturing established in the UK over the period would therefore have amounted to some £937 m. As against this, Professor Remmers shows (from UK official sources) that total expenditure over the period by British-quoted companies in manufacturing was £10,910 m. Thus, the share of fixed asset expenditure by foreign companies out of the total foreign and indigenous expenditure in manufacturing in Britain over that period was some 7·9 per cent.

Further valuable data has been collected by Professor John H. Dunning in his book *Studies in International Investment*, published in 1970. The following table, taken from the book,[16] shows plant and equipment expenditures by United States subsidiaries in the EEC and in the United Kingdom as a percentage of gross domestic fixed capital formation in those countries. The figures broadly bear out the result reported above for the United Kingdom, and show substantially smaller percentages for other European countries for the period from 1957 to 1965.

Plant and Equipment Expenditure by US Subsidiaries
as Percentage of all Gross Domestic Fixed Capital Formation[17]

	1957	1959	1961	1963	1965
Belgium	2·2	2·6	3·3	3·8	4·5
France	1·8	1·9	2·1	3·0	4·0
West Germany	1·8	2·9	4·2	3·9	4·1
Italy	2·0	1·3	2·9	4·1	5·0
Netherlands	2·6	1·2	3·2	5·4	4·8
EEC	2·2	2·6	3·3	3·8	4·5
United Kingdom	7·8	5·7	7·4	7·9	10·0

SOURCE: *Economic Bulletin for Europe*, Vol. 19, Nov. 1967, page 67. US Department of Commerce, *Survey of Current Business*, Nov. 1966, page 8, and OECD Main Economic Indicators, various issues.

[16] John H. Dunning, *Studies in International Investment*, George Allen & Unwin Ltd., London, 1970. Page 306, Table 18.
[17] In machinery and equipment.

In another work[18] Professor Dunning also showed 'expenditure on plant and equipment by US firms in manufacturing and petroleum' as a percentage of 'gross fixed capital formation' in the period 1957 to 1965.

Expenditure on plant and equipment by US firms in manufacturing and petroleum as a percentage of gross fixed capital formation in UK industry

1957	1958	1959	1960	1961	1962	1963	1964	1965
10·0	9·5	7·4	7·3	9·1	8·5	9·9	9·6	11·5

As will be seen, the percentages shown varied from 11·5 per cent, the highest, to 7·3 per cent, the lowest. The fact that the percentages are slightly higher than those quoted above derives probably from the fact that the British-based oil companies are excluded from the British data.

CONCLUSIONS TO PART I

The main themes emerging from the whole of the foregoing may perhaps be summed up as follows. Except in some cases of short- and long-term borrowing in certain countries, the whole scope of international companies' financial operations, both as regards national capital resources and international balance of payments flows, form a very small proportion of total transactions. This is presumably because international companies, however large they might appear in comparison with other companies, still form a small component in the massive turnover of national and international capital as a whole.

Secondly, it emerges that as a matter of economic principle, direct investment flows are beneficial both to the originator and the host countries. This follows from the fact that international investment flows, like analogous flows within country borders, serve the purpose of creating new business enterprises, which themselves generate new profit and capital resources. The latter in course of time attain larger dimensions than either the capital outflows or income inflows of the parent, and thus alternately benefit the balance of payments of the parent's country and the volume of capital resources of the affiliate's country.

[18] John H. Dunning, *The Role of American Investment in the British Economy*, PEP Broadsheet 507, February 1969, page 120, Table 1.

PART II

Financial Management

CHAPTER 4

The Task of
International Financial Management

The foregoing Part I has considered international enterprise as a whole, and has attempted to assess its overall effect on the total financial and economic environment in which it works; that is to say, on the total capital resources and on the cross-frontier flows of capital and income of the countries in which international corporations operate. The view taken of international companies has thus been objective in the sense that they have been regarded as a collective entity, exerting a common force, and having common consequences.

It is now necessary to turn to a subjective examination. The present Part will consider the financing of international enterprise from the standpoint of the companies themselves; that is to say, it will examine the manner in which companies approach the subject of financial management, and will attempt to identify the problems which they encounter and the manner in which they solve them. In the course of this examination the effect on the outside world will not be disregarded. The overall effect of international companies' financing has already been quantified in the previous Part; however, the principles of financial conduct adopted by international companies, and the methods utilised by them, lead to the formation of general judgements about international companies which may be sympathetic or otherwise to the objects which they pursue. Moreover, the day-to-day operation of the finances of these companies will have effects in certain exogenous areas such as that of short-term capital movements, which have not been quantified in Part I and which will require examination in the present Part.

Three basic points require exposition at the outset.

(a) The Independence of the Financial Services

The proper discharge of the financial services' functions is, of course, crucial to the welfare of the company as a whole. However, it is important to maintain this role in realistic perspective—in particular, the degree of autonomy available to the financial service should not be overstated. The conduct of the financial business of a company is one of the components of the overall functioning of the enterprise, others of which include production, marketing, research, and labour management. It cannot be stated that the financial services have a power of initiative or of overriding action, as against these other main components. Indeed, the proposition might be made that the essential function of a company lies in its production and marketing activities, whilst the functions of finance and, for example, research, and labour relations, are complementary rather than central to the operation of the business.

A consideration of the individual financial items to be managed will serve to illustrate this point.

If the various headings of the company flow of funds, as analysed in the foregoing Part, are taken in turn, the degree of prerogative accruing to the financial manager can be assessed. The sources of funds of a company consist, as is known, of cash flow—which is sub-divided again into net profits after tax, and provisions for depreciation; of bank credit, owners' equity, long-term liabilities, trade credit, and decreases in liquid assets.

Of these, the internal financing flow—profits after tax, and depreciation provisions—is clearly determined by factors and processes beyond the original control of the financial service. The earnings of a company are ultimately decided by the level of demand in the overall economy for its products, and by the success of the marketing division of the company in exploiting this potential. The company's earnings would at the same time reflect the balance between revenue from sales, and the cost of production and of other items of expenditure; the latter are conditional upon the economic organisation of the production processes—the maintenance of technological standards and of maximum economy in the use of labour and materials, and the best possible exploitation of research results, etc. The earnings which go into cash flow are in themselves net of taxation, the latter being determined by national and local authorities beyond the control of company financial services. Similarly, depreciation provisions are contingent upon the level of earnings on the one hand, and the level of investment deemed suitable on the other; the latter is determined, again, by future prospects for production and marketing determined by the company's management as a whole.

The resort to external financing is, in the last resort, a function of the self-financing capacity of the company, or in other words, of its sales and earning capacity. Where external financing comes into play, the financial services of the company certainly have a responsibility for recommending what form this should take; whether it should be short-term bank credit, longer-term borrowing, or the recruitment of new equity capital. Here again, however, factors external to the financial services will exert a significant influence. The capacity of a company to recruit capital, either in the form of equity or long-term borrowing, is dependent on the reputation of the company in the capital market; this, in its turn, results from the profit and sales record previously established. Similarly, the availability of bank credit will be determined, at least to some extent, by the money supply policy of the economy in which the company is operating, and the choice as between various forms of credit, long- and short-term, will be further conditioned by the structure of interest rates. All in all, the function of the financial department in the practice of external financing will be an advisory and managerial, rather than an instigatory one.

The uses of company funds can be sub-divided into the main heading of: dividend payments, expenditure on fixed assets, payments of interest, royalties, management fees, etc., extension of trade credit, investment in fixed assets, and increase in liquid assets. The dividend outlay depends clearly, in the first instance, on the level of earnings, but regardless of the former, the dividend policy of the typical company is determined at least as much by long-term considerations of the company's standing and attraction to shareholders, as by its immediate financial position. Expenditure on fixed assets meets with considerations similar to those remarked upon in regard to depreciation. This expenditure is pre-conditioned by the sales prospects of the company, and its existing earnings performance. Management fees and royalties proceed from operational and technological aspects of the company's activities not within the direct control of the finance department. Trade credit arises from marketing exigencies; an increase in liquid assets tends to be a residual of the above items.

Thus although the finance department's role is a crucial one—particularly where such matters as future investment are under examination—it is not, as the above review illustrates, an overriding one. The activities of an industrial company essentially set up flows of resources which flow from production to sales, and thence back through research, marketing, and investment, to further production. At various points in this flow the resources will be translated, if only briefly, into financial forms, and it is with these that the finance department is charged. The function of the finance department, therefore, is to manage, conserve, and dispose to optimum advantage the resources of the company which come into its trust in financial form.

(b) The Multi-Company Group

The foregoing is an outline of the intrinsic activities and responsibilities of financial management of any company, and it is of course a simplified statement applying to the company as a notional single entity.

However, this basic concept is subject to an immediate complication in the case of the type of company under consideration in the present study, since the latter is not a single corporate body, but a group of entities each having a separate corporate identity. This means that the basic company function, that of production and sale of a given product, is not an homogeneous but a multiple activity, and that there is not a single but several flows of resources in progress within the group. The counterpart to this is that there are several financial streams requiring separate financial management. It becomes, therefore, the task of the group financial services to co-ordinate the whole of this diverse activity.

Clearly, the end object of group management will be to further the financial viability and profitability of the parent company, the originator of the total group activity, and the owner of the subsidiary companies in question. The fulfilment of this purpose will, however, require a careful blend of centralisation and of disaggregation. A proper degree of autonomy on the part of the subsidiary companies will be required, partly because of the divergent activities in which they are engaged and in which they only can be expert, and indeed, where their financial needs will be disparate; and partly because of their very existence as separate corporate structures, having therefore individual rights and duties under company law.

In practice, the pattern of financial management will tend to work out in the following manner. The recruitment of proceeds from production and sales and its reallocation to subsequent users will now take the form, not of the appropriation of revenue from a single production and sales mechanism, but of the harnessing of the several revenues of a number of production and sales flows. This means that, in effect, the multiple earnings of the individual companies will be commuted through the medium of profit transfers into a group cash flow to be redispensed within the group, and to outside claimants such as shareholders and creditors, according to the group management's judgement. However, there are many intervening factors in this process. The subsidiary company profits furnished to group headquarters will themselves be the product of external as well as internal financing on the part of the subsidiaries. In this respect, the common practice will tend to be for shorter-term external financing such as bank credit, to be conducted virtually independently by a subsidiary company's management, whereas longer-term financing such as the issue of bonds and the acquisition of equity capital will be made on the authority, and frequently in the name, of the parent company. Allied with this function is the prerogative of the parent company in almost all cases to allow or disallow investment projects. Thus, as a matter of general principle, whereas the subsidiary is responsible for current earnings and short-term external finance, the parent company takes upon itself the main strategic dispositions of the company's finance: the distribution of group profits, the acquisition of fresh capital, the internal allocation of group cash flow, and the determination of group long-term investment.

However, the above outline understates practical difficulties involved in the work of co-ordination. In the first place, the intercorporate structure necessarily embraces a variety of individual aims, preferences and apprehensions. The degree of reconciliation required for a headquarters/subsidiary agreement on the level of profit transfers, of fixed asset investment, or of short-term, as distinct from long-term, external financing, will be evident. At the lowest level, a common definition of the financial aggregates under management—the valuation of stocks and work in progress, the terms and conditions of bank borrowing, the extent of liquid assets, the liability to tax, etc., will not be easy to find. Still less easy will be the consolidation of company accounts—if not on a balance sheet basis, certainly on a flow of funds basis.

Secondly, the position will be complicated by the fact of the subsidiaries' existence as separate companies. This means that their accounts are separately exposed to official control and to revenue impositions alongside those of the parent company. Thus, the simple movement of funds from one location to another, as is possible within the confines of a single company, is not possible between the members of an intercorporate group. Monies can be transferred only in the manner decreed by company law. In brief, this restricts the transmission of funds to the remittance of profits and the establishment of intra-company liabilities; it is apparent from this that the only method of permanent transfer is through the medium of profits and equity capital contributions. Substantial displacements of funds can be achieved through loans, trade credit, etc., but these must of course, to satisfy company account requirements, be repaid in due course. It will be apparent, at this point, that the claims of public revenue both add to the complexity and reduce the volume of transfers of the resources in question. Subsidiary company profits available for transfer to the parent company are themselves net of tax imposed on their subsidiaries' own earnings. The passage of dividends to the parent is subject to tax on distributions, although this may in most cases be reduced or commuted. The parent company's profits are also liable for tax, and its distribution of dividends are liable again for taxation. In addition, interest payable on intra-company loans is liable for tax in the hands of the recipient, although it is deductible from the earnings of the paying company.

The foregoing attempts only to sketch in some of the consequences attendant upon the organisation of industrial activity in the form of multi-company groups. As will be seen, the outcome so affects financial management as to make it not only substantially more complex than in the case of single companies, but also somewhat different in nature.

(*c*) *The International Posture*

The multi-company group is by no means an exclusively international phenomenon. Indeed, it emerged within the framework of national economies, and is a well-known form of company structure within the boundaries of individual countries. In fact, there are almost certainly very many more multi-company groups at work inside countries, and having no international affiliations, than there are multi-company groups of an explicitly international character. The present study is concerned, however, only with the latter category.

The distinctive characteristic of international companies is that the subsidiary companies, with all their relationships to the parent company described in the above section, are all placed in separate countries. This adds a new dimension to the considerations brought forward above. Not only are the subsidiaries of international parents separate corporate structures in their own right, subject to official accounting procedures, company legislation, and revenue impositions, but they are subject to these effects, not under the same national law as the parent company, but under all the separate and frequently conflicting laws of the various individual countries in which the subsidiaries are located.

The separation of national law is worthy perhaps of emphasis at this point (as has already been mentioned in Part I, pp. 12–13). The notion of an international company as a body detached from, or indeed superior to, the supervision and control of national governments is, at least in the financial and legal sense, not applicable. The subsidiaries of a multi-national parent company are each separate national companies registered in the country of their location, and subject to the company law and all other financial and economic regulations of that country. The parent company, in its turn, is a national of its own country where it is registered, and where it similarly is subject to the company law and financial and economic regulations of that country. The cases listed at the foot of page 13 of Part I are those where, for administrative convenience, it has been decided to set up two parent companies in separate countries. This has, however, not lessened the degree of government supervision of parent company activity; on the contrary, it appears to have substituted dual for single supervision.

The broad effects of this multiplicity of national jurisdictions and environments can be summarised as follows. In the first place, the individual operation of each of the subsidiaries and of the parent company will be subject to differing company laws. These will affect the disclosure of company affairs and financial data in the company report and accounts; they will also affect the appointment of directors, the voting rights of shareholders, the nominal capital and other company affairs, in which, of course, the parent company as the sole or major shareholder will be closely involved. The broader financial regulation of the country of operation of the subsidiary will also determine the level of its local borrowing, both short- and long-term. Special provisions may apply to the financing of foreign-owned companies through locally-raised capital, and may prescribe minimum levels of imported equity. In a broader sense, the local regulation of money supply, the structure of interest rates, and the development of the capital market—which, as remarked in the foregoing, influenced the nature of external financing—will differ in each country where a subsidiary of the group exists. More broadly still, the movement of the general economy and the development of the market for the group's products, affecting as these do the earnings and cash flow position of the company, will vary from country to country in which the subsidiaries of the group are located. For its part, the parent company will be subject to its own national company law as regards registration, disclosure, the maintenance of company accounts, the appointment of officers, voting procedure, the issue of capital, and the constitution of company funds.

Apart from the question of surveillance and official control, the international group will be subject to the varying taxation systems of each of the countries in which it has established subsidiaries. The earnings of each of the individual subsidiaries will thus reflect different rates of profit, and the distribution of these profits will be subject to different rates of tax. Allowances for expenditure items will differ, and the definition of these items will vary from country to country. More particularly, investment conditions will vary. Allowances against tax for depreciation provisions—for an essential item, therefore, in cash flow—will be dissimilar; and incentives for investment either in grant or tax rebate form will vary not only from country to country, but from region to region within countries.

So much for the disparate control and taxation conditions affecting the internal operation of the subsidiaries and the parent company in their respective countries. When the question of transactions between the subsidiaries and the parent company are considered, then a further multiplicity of controls and taxation systems come into question. Restrictions on exports of capital circumscribe the ability of the parent to provide equity to the subsidiaries. The restrictions on the remittance of profit to non-resident recipients may also limit the level of profit remittances possible for the subsidiary: this effect may be compounded by a requirement on the part of the national authorities of the parent company for a minimum level of profit receipts in respect of the capital exported. There are also various provisions as to the volume of borrowing and lending across frontiers, and as to the disposal of the proceeds of such transactions. It has already been mentioned that the level of local borrowing by subsidiaries—which is a matter of concern to the parent company—may be subject to regulation. In a slightly broader context, there is a degree of supervision by the various customs authorities of the countries concerned of the level of prices at which goods are exchanged between members of multi-company groups. Transactions between members of international groups are, of course, subject to tax. The transfer of profits from subsidiaries to parents are liable, as are the receipts of interest on loans. The levels of such taxes will vary from country to country, and will also vary according to whether double taxation treaties have been concluded between the countries concerned.

In addition to the above, transactions between multinational company groups are subject to the vagaries of the exchange rates of the various currencies used.

Finally, a range of national contingencies such as nationalisation, expropriation, compulsory share participation, compulsory profit levels, dividend payouts, wage levels, local material purchasing, export or import quotas are operable; and beyond these there remain the dangers of loss, either partial or complete, through war or civil commotion.

In all, as will be seen, the inherent complications of the financial management of a multi-company group are sizeably enlarged where this group has an international character. These complications proceed from the simple variety of national legislations and prescriptions in force; but also, it should be noted, from the existence of restrictions and controls specifically in position owing to the existence of international multi-company groups.

(d) Conclusion

Three major comments appear to arise from the points outlined above. The first is that of the three main characteristics of the companies in question, which have been enumerated, the first two are those of any company, and not solely of international companies. They are therefore of less interest to the present study, which will be directed primarily to the implications arising out of the third characteristic. However, some aspects of company financial management per se qualify the particular operation of international companies discussed below, and will be introduced where required.

The second point is that the concept of an international company, or indeed of any company, as a corporate body concentrating in the hands of its financial manager large quantities of funds which may be shifted and employed as virtually freely available financial assets at will, does not appear to correspond to reality. The flows of resources in any company are primarily devoted to the physical functions of production (either of goods or services), sales and investment in which the company is engaged, and unattached financial assets are not a normal feature of these companies.

The third main conclusion appears to be that the adoption of international operations implies, for the financial management of a company, a considerable accretion of complications and impediments. It appears evident that the move to international activity would not, in the greatest probability, be undertaken if financial considerations were solely at issue. Companies expand across frontiers for evident purposes of manufacturing and distribution improvement. The effect for the financial services is to add to their tasks, rather than to facilitate their freedom of action.

These conclusions serve to predetermine the lines upon which the ensuing study of the financial management of international corporations should be pursued. The fact that the international corporation is primarily a producing and selling entity of the multi-company group category, such as is to be found in normal business life, irrespective of whether this be national or international in character, serves to narrow down the area to be explored. A number of attributes frequently noted in international companies are those which it possesses by virtue of its role as a multi-company group, rather than as an international company. For example, the preference for 100%-owned subsidiaries, for the provision to the subsidiary of loan rather than equity capital, for the control by the parent company of the subsidiaries' investment policy, and for fluctuating dividend payments from year to year by the subsidiaries, are attributes of multi-company groups rather than specifically of international companies. Conversely, some advantages ascribed to international companies remain in doubt, owing to the limitations to which the international enterprise is subject as a normal producing and selling company. For example, the supposition that international companies, as such, have greater liquid funds to circulate within the group, appears improbable in the light of the intrinsic restraints outlined above, lying upon the financial services of any industrial and commercial company.

What follows will therefore attempt to discuss the features of financial management which are exclusive to and wholly consequential upon the international nature of the companies under consideration in the present study. The field to be surveyed remains large and highly variegated, and it appears necessary to consider the data under headings sufficiently few and embracing to allow of consistent examination. The themes most appropriate for this purpose appear to be those of (i) taxation; (ii) exchange risk; and (iii) the recruitment of capital.

CHAPTER 5

Taxation

(*a*) THE CONCEPT OF INTERNATIONAL TAX LIABILITY

The essence of the multi-company group is that it consists of separate corporate bodies all engaged in the process of production for profit. Necessarily, and with justice, these profits are taxable. However, a loss, which may be rightly considered anomalous, arises if the profits of the subsidiary, once acquitted of their company taxation charge, are, when remitted to the parent company—the sole owner of that subsidiary—then subjected to a further and equal tax as the profits, in their turn, of the parent company. This occurrence would constitute double taxation in accordance with the formal definition of the latter, i.e. where the appropriate tax jurisdiction or jurisdictions impose tax twice in respect of the same taxable event and person.[1]

(*i*) *International Double Taxation*

The principle of the impropriety of double taxation is well recognised by the taxation law of most countries where multi-company groups exist. In most cases dividends, when paid by one corporate body to another corporate body having a prescribed minimum participation in the share capital of that body, are free of company taxation. However, as soon as intercorporate company activity extends beyond the boundaries of a single country, the position changes. The national taxation laws of few, if any, countries recognise a right of a foreign parent company to receive profits from a domestically-based subsidiary free of company tax applicable to the profits of that subsidiary in the country in question. On the contrary, a number of countries, having once taxed the profits of the subsidiary, apply a further withholding tax to the dividends of that subsidiary when distributed to the foreign parent company, on the general grounds that the dividends are profits lost to the country in question, and that some recouping of the latter should be ensured. It is left to the operation

[1] Barry Spitz, *International Tax Planning*, London, Butterworths, 1972.

of double taxation treaties concluded between the country of the subsidiary and the country of the parent company, and to the relief devices provided by the revenue authorities of the parent company, to mitigate some of the effects of the application of this principle.

(ii) Relief of Double Taxation

In principle, the combined effect of the two procedures mentioned above effects the same relief for the international parent company as it does for the multi-company parent within national borders. In the latter case the underlying tax, i.e. the tax on the undistributed profits of the subsidiary, is deemed to have been paid by the parent; that is to say the subsidiary's dividends, when taken into the parent company's funds, are immune to the subsequent tax on the parent company's undistributed profits. Double taxation treaties and tax credits granted by national governments to international company parents in principle duplicate this process. The tax credit grants relief from the primary taxation on the subsidiary company's profits; clearly, the government of the host country is unable to perform this function, since such reliefs must be claimed by the recipient of dividends, and the latter is in this case outside the purview of the national revenue authorities. Thus the process of multi-company group income franking is separated, by the inherent nature of international companies, between different national taxation authorities. Double taxation treaties serve to remove the withholding tax levied, as mentioned above, on the payment outside national borders of subsidiaries' dividends; this tax derives essentially from the international nature of the enterprise, and would not, of course, arise in the case of dividend payments by resident subsidiaries to resident parents.

However, the above describes only the broad intention of relief procedures against the double taxation of international companies. The complementary operations of the two national revenue authorities concerned do not, in many cases, coincide. The tax base of one country may not be recognised by the authorities of the other. A well-known example is provided by the pioneer reliefs and regional tax incentives given to subsidiary companies, but not recognised by the tax authorities of the parent. Where tax liabilities and immunities enjoy equal recognition on both sides, the scope of such taxes may be differently interpreted. Expenses and allowances may be variously defined and variously computed. Double taxation agreements do not always provide for the full remission of withholding taxes, a proportion of which may continue to be levied. In this case, an appropriate credit may or may not be allowed by the revenue authorities of the parent company.

Above all it is important to note that where the underlying tax rate exceeds that of the parent country, no relief in any case is normally granted. Some revenue authorities in this case permit an averaging of tax burdens suffered by subsidiaries in all foreign countries for the purpose of assessing the parent company's tax credit; but other revenue authorities apply a per country limitation. Per contra, where the total tax liability of the subsidiary is a lower percentage rate than that applied in the parent country, then the parent company will nevertheless pay the full home rate on receiving the subsidiary's dividends into its own profits.

Again, some parent tax jurisdictions, in order to encourage overseas investment, go beyond granting full relief on foreign income and give further relief on the parent's overall tax bill in proportion to the foreign income element included.

Clearly, innumerable possibilities arise: from the extreme position in which no double taxation agreement exists and no tax credits on foreign income are allowed by the parent government, and in which subsidiaries' profits taken into the parent company's profits are thus taxed twice—to the opposite extreme in which an actual abatement of the parent company's total tax bill is granted in consideration of the foreign element in its aggregate incomes. The majority of cases, however, will fall within the middle spectrum, in which subsidiaries' tax charges will be allowable against the parent's tax liability. Definitional differences will, however, lead frequently to a net addition to the parent's tax liability under its home jurisdiction. Above all—even where full equivalence is achieved in relating the scope and nature of the foreign tax to the tax prescriptions of the parent country—should the overall tax liability of the subsidiary company be greater than that of the parent company, then the margin of tax charges arising must be paid by the parent company over and above the habitual domestic level. Also, where the tax rate incumbent upon the subsidiary is less than that upon the parent, the latter will pay tax at its domestic rate on the subsidiary's profit which it receives.

(iii) A Numerical Model

It is convenient, at this stage, to summarise the above by means of simplified figures.

Where a parent company has total profits of £200, and these profits comprise £100 of its own earnings and £100 of the earnings of its foreign subsidiary transmitted in the form of dividends, and where the full rate of corporate tax in the parent country is 50 per cent, then the parent company will necessarily wish to pay in tax 50 per cent of the consolidated income, or £100. This can only arise where the foreign taxation imposed on the foreign subsidiary's profit is accredited, through the medium of double taxation treaties and tax credits, as prepaid tax in the country of the parent company. The process is as follows:

The foreign subsidiary's profits of £100 are taxed by the foreign taxation authorities at 50 per cent, viz. £50: the sum of £50 is received by the parent company as pretaxed dividends from the subsidiary. This is recognised as such by the revenue authorities of the parent country. The parent company then declares £150 of profit to its revenue authorities, of which £50 is 'franked' (i.e. tax has already been paid) and attracts no further tax charge. The revenue authorities of the parent country then levy 50 per cent, or £50, on the remaining £100. The parent has struck a total profit of £200, and has paid a tax charge of 50 per cent, or £100, on this total.

Should double taxation agreements and tax credits not be available, then double taxation will occur, viz. the foreign subsidiary pays a 50 per cent tax charge to the foreign revenue authorities, and transmits £50 in dividends to the parent company. These dividends are not accredited as tax-paid income of the parent company. The parent company declares £150 consolidated profits to its own revenue authorities, no claim as to franked income lying. The revenue authorities of the parent country then charge 50 per cent of £150, i.e. £75. Thus on the total profits of the group of £200, a combined tax of £125 has been paid, leaving the group with £75. This tax burden arises as follows. The subsidiary company's profit of £100 is taxed as to £50 by the subsidiary company's revenue authorities; the remaining £50 is taxed again as to £25 by the revenue authorities of the parent company. The parent company's profits of £100 are taxed as to £50 by the revenue authorities of that company.

Effective reduction of the parent company's tax burden by reason of the existence of income from abroad would occur where a lower rate of parent country taxation was applied to the foreign element in the parent company's consolidated profit, in conjunction with a tax credit for foreign taxation. Thus a foreign subsidiary's profit of £100 would be taxed as to £50 by the foreign revenue authorities, and the resulting remittance of £50 in dividends to the parent company would be deemed by the revenue authorities of the parent company as attracting a tax credit, not equivalent to but greater than the foreign tax paid. Thus where the tax credit given were, for example, £60, the resultant overall tax burden on the parent company would be reduced from £100 to £95.

Within the first case illustrated above, i.e. that of tax remissionable foreign income within the normal spectrum of experience, there are, as explained above, two classes of cases in which the foreign tax charged is not relieved precisely pro rata. In the first case the foreign tax charge may be greater than the tax charge of the parent country, in which case an excess of tax is payable by the parent company; the second case is that in which the foreign tax charge is lower than the tax charge of the parent company, and in this instance the parent company pays its full domestic tax regardless of the lower underlying tax on its foreign income.

These two cases each fall into two possible alternatives.

In the first place, as stated above, the method of calculation of the foreign taxable income and tax base may differ as between the foreign revenue authorities and those of the parent company. Thus the foreign revenue authorities may assess the foreign subsidiary's taxable income at £100, whereas under the criteria applicable by the parent company's revenue authorities, this income may be £110. These dividends would then be charged by the parent company's revenue authorities at:

$$£\frac{110}{100} \times 50 = £55$$

thus creating a net additional tax burden to the consolidated profits of £5. On the other hand, the foreign revenue authorities might assess the subsidiary company's taxable income at £110, whereas those of the parent company calculated it at £100. In this case, an additional £5 of net consolidated tax would arise, deriving, in this instance, from extra tax paid to the foreign revenue authorities.

In the other major alternative the rates of corporation tax in the two countries might differ; thus where the rate applied by the revenue authorities of the parent company was 50 per cent, that in the foreign country might be either above or below this level; i.e. it might, for instance, be 60 per cent or 40 per cent. In the first instance the foreign company's profit of £100 would be reduced by £60, the remaining £40 taken into the profit of the parent company. This would be 'franked', but at a rate only of 50 per cent. Thus the parent company would pay tax of £50 on its own earnings of £100, and tax of £60 on the foreign company's earnings of £100 would have been paid. Total tax on the £200 profit of the group would be £110, or 55 per cent. In the other alternative, tax of £40 would be paid by the subsidiary company, but on its inclusion in the parent company's profits it would be liable to a 50 per cent tax, of which only 40 per cent was 'franked'. Thus the group as a whole would still pay £100 on the consolidated profit of £200, although the tax rates of the two national revenue authorities were 50 per cent and 40 per cent; i.e. an implicit £90 on the £200 profit.

(b) CONCLUSIONS ON INTERNATIONAL TAX LIABILITY

All of the above can be summarised under two general comments:

(i) The two extreme cases cited above, i.e. of full double taxation, and of an actual reduction of parent company taxation, are sufficiently special as not to require further treatment in the present context. Cases of tax benefits from the ownership of subsidiary companies are so rare as to permit of their being disregarded. Cases of full double taxation normally fail to arise, since, in practice companies do not, in such taxation circumstances, establish subsidiary companies abroad.

(ii) Save in the rare case mentioned above, it emerges from the foregoing that parent companies always pay at least the full rate of taxation on their consolidated profits, constituted by their own earnings and the repatriated dividends of their foreign subsidiaries. Where the tax rates on subsidiary company profits are below the parent company tax rates, then the parent company pays the full domestic rate; where the subsidiary company's tax rates are above the parent country tax rates, then the parent company pays the additional charge. (Under some national taxation systems the alternative higher ceiling is differently disposed, but the net effect is unchanged.)

It follows that attention must now be given to the reaction of international companies to this situation.

(c) COMPANY TREATMENT OF INTERNATIONAL TAXATION

Two preliminary observations are required.

(i) Continuing Vigilance

In the first place it is to be expected, in the light of the above, that companies should devote a good deal of attention to the problem of taxation. The double taxation of income, whether that of physical or legal persons, has for very many years been a proper subject of fiscal concern, and the taxation legislation of most countries has been specifically designed to eliminate this phenomenon. The parents of international companies are therefore normally anxious to ensure that protection from double taxation should not be breached in their case owing solely to the geographical accident that the component companies of their group are located in several tax jurisdictions, rather than in one. The point, if kept closely in view, can be significant for the overall revenues of the group. With appropriate legal and accounting investigation and clarification, conflicts between separate national tax jurisdictions which might involve substantial revenue charges upon the parent can frequently be reconciled. The international companies should be, and indeed are, vigilant observers of the changing tax conditions of the countries in which they operate, and of the opportunities presented them for minimising their tax burden.

(ii) No Tax Avoidance

On the other hand, however, it remains a matter of recorded fact that international companies do not necessarily make specific adjustments in their financial affairs for the sole object of avoiding or reducing their tax burden. In his study of practice in thirty American corporations with European subsidiaries, Professor Lee Remmers[2] observed that only a quarter of these reported that they assigned 'the highest importance to the tax consideration', and that between 50 per cent and 60 per cent of the sample did not go so far as to give 'considerable' attention to the

[2] *op. cit.* page 60.

subject. There may well be two reasons for this attitude to the subject. Firstly, this may reflect the reasonably smooth functioning of double taxation and tax credit arrangements, particularly as between the United States and the European countries in which the subsidiaries were located. Although this may be a fairly significant factor, it remains true that this would not cover situations where the tax charge on subsidiaries was at a higher or lower rate than that applicable in the United States. The second reason may therefore be that many companies accept tax discrepancies— save where they appear in extreme forms—as a necessary accompaniment to the process of transacting international business. Overseas investment necessarily carries with it certain additional costs; inter alia those of the recruitment of specialist staff; of multilingual promotional activities; of greater deviations from standardised manufacture, etc.; among these extra costs may perhaps be counted the supplementary burden of being subjected to differing tax liabilities. This may be particularly true of international companies operating in the new industrial centres of the Western Hemisphere, where corporate tax rates are increasingly convergent. Other companies may well feel that the tax situation is so changeable and so little open to prediction, that tax avoidance activities are a diseconomy in themselves.

However this may be, it remains necessary to consider the ways in which companies may optimise their international tax position. As mentioned in the foregoing, international companies' primary recourse no doubt lies in the constant attention they give to the international taxation theme, and the efforts they make to reconcile the legal and accounting points of difference that arise. Other courses, however, remain open.

It is apparent from the foregoing that double taxation only arises on the payment of dividends by the subsidiary to its parent. This introduces an important preliminary point. Avoidance of dividend payments, or substitution of these payments by the other forms mentioned in the following pages, recommends itself as a practical recourse only where the tax rate of the subsidiary is below that of the parent. Where the tax rate is higher, the subsidiary's dividends when remitted to the parent will incur tax relief up to the parent's rate—the margin remaining irrecoverable. When the subsidiary's tax rate is lower, then remittance to the parent will convert the tax liability to a higher total. Thus in the first case the higher tax is, and remains, paid wherever the profits are directed. In the second, the higher of the two possible rates only operates from the moment the profits are transferred to the parent. This suggests the merit, at least in theory, of the principle of concentration of group profits in areas of lowest taxation.

(iii) Nil Dividend Remittances

It follows immediately from this that there can be an argument in principle in favour of refraining from remitting profits from the subsidiary to the parent, and of retaining them as undistributed earnings within the former. This course is commonly resorted to in any case by international companies for the financing of new asset formation. It is self evident that no financial benefit results from the financing of subsidiaries' new assets by fresh equity capital from the parent, where the latter derives at least in part from profit remittances of the subsidiary taxed below the parent's nominal rate.

Another recourse would lie in the routeing of the subsidiary's profits, not to the parent company, but to another company in the group located in another country, where tax considerations may be more favourable. However, it is important to notice that company law in most countries would prohibit the simple payment of dividends to another operating subsidiary elsewhere. The dividend payment in question could only be made to an international holding company which would itself require to hold sufficient shares in the subsidiary as to make it the legal owner of that company. This method will be further discussed below.

There are, however, natural limitations on the extent to which dividend remittances can be withheld from the parent, either for use by the subsidiary or for transmission to other parts of the group. It is inherent to the operation of the multi-company group that profits should accrue eventually to the parent. Should these fail to materialise for an unduly long period, then the existence of the multi-company group is necessarily brought into hazard. In the case of the international multi-company group, this practical factor emerges at a fairly early stage. Given the reluctance with which a number of governments view the expatriation of profits by subsidiaries located in their territory, it is often important to establish a regular remittance policy for fear that the exchange control authorities might, after a lengthy period of unpaid dividends, intervene to disallow their resumption. Governmental pressure on international companies' freedom of action, tending to the same effect, comes from an equal and opposite direction. The governments of a number of capital-exporting countries, among them the us and the uk, require either formally or informally that a given percentage of subsidiaries' total earnings should be remitted to the parent in the form of dividends.

All in all, therefore, it appears likely that the combined effect of the above factors upon international companies' dividend remittance policies is neutral. This appears to be borne out in the figures. As will be seen from the chart on page 61 in Part I, Professor Remmers found that the dividend payout of a sample of foreign-owned subsidiaries operating in the uk, when expressed as a percentage of total uses of funds, to be very similar to that of British-quoted companies (22 per cent as against 20 per cent). Perhaps the apposite ratio is the dividend payout as a percentage of net profit after tax. Professor Remmers[3] shows that this was 56 per cent for foreign subsidiaries in the UK as against 52 per cent for British-quoted companies. He also shows[4] that the payout ratio was higher for American-owned companies than for European-owned companies (median value percentage 51 per cent for American subsidiaries; 45 per cent for European subsidiaries).

The *Survey of Current Business*[5] shows dividend remittances of US manufacturing subsidiaries abroad—'earnings', less 'reinvested earnings' —to be 54·3 per cent of total profits in 1967 and 1968, as compared with a ratio of 57·1 per cent for domestically-based United States companies in manufacturing.[6] Similarly, British figures[7] show that the payout ratio of British-owned subsidiaries in North America and Western Europe in the period 1963–67 was 48·6 per cent, which compares fairly closely with the ratio noted above for British companies in the UK. British-owned subsidiaries in the developing world show a payout ratio of 42·3 per cent in the same period. Similarly, foreign subsidiaries in the United States in the period 1967 to 1968 showed a payout ratio of just over 32 per cent[8] within which was incorporated a payout ratio on British subsidiaries alone of 38 per cent.

The above data seems to reflect a variation in payout ratios according to criteria of investment maturity and origin of parent as suggested in Part I of the present study. New investments, i.e. those mainly of continental European countries, and investment in relatively less profitable areas such as the developing countries, show a comparatively low payout ratio; long-established subsidiaries, particularly in areas of higher profitability such as North America and Western Europe, show relatively high payout ratios. These payout ratios, moreover, tend to reproduce those habitual to all companies in the country of the parent. In this, the tendency of the parent company—in common with those of all multi-company groups—to require from its subsidiaries a profit return sufficient to support its own dividend policy, is evident.

(iv) Substitution of Dividends by Other Payments

It follows from the above that insofar as there is no deliberate avoidance of dividend payments, there can logically be no replacement of such absent dividends by other means of payment.

[3] *op. cit.* page 310.
[4] *op. cit.* page 309.
[5] *Survey of Current Business*, October 1968, pp. 23 and 24, and October 1969, pp. 28 and 29.
[6] *Survey of Current Business*, July 1971, pp. 38 and 39.
[7] *Business Monitor M4*, 1971, Table 4.
[8] *Survey of Current Business*, October 1969, p. 35.

However, there are in principle a number of channels through which subsidiary profits might be transferred to the parent; the merits of these should be examined, and the conclusions to which this investigation appears to lead can then be tested against both the above and other numerical data.

The object of dividend-avoiding procedures is, as stated above, to transfer the resources of the subsidiary company to the parent in such a form that it does not attract the taxation of the host country; i.e. that it is not considered a distribution of profit. This can be achieved in one of two main ways. Resources can be transferred in forms which the taxation authorities recognise as costs against operating revenues before a trading profit is established; i.e. in the form of payment of royalties to the parent company for the use of processes patented by the latter, and of management and other technical service fees payable to the parent company. Alternatively, the resources can be transferred on an allocation of total income which is not subject to corporate taxation, i.e. as interest on loan capital.

One general remark regarding the tax-avoiding potential of these two procedures is necessary. The transfers are not deemed to be part of the taxable profits of the subsidiary, and are therefore exempt from the taxation of the host country. However, on their receipt by the parent company they are deemed by the revenue authorities of that country to be an income of the company, and as such, fully taxable. The treatment of fees and loan interest in the hands of the parent company is no different from that of dividends. At this point it must be recalled that, as stated above, double taxation and tax credit arrangements effectively relieve the parent company of foreign taxation levied on its receipt of dividends. The tax advantage of converting subsidiary companies' earnings from dividends into fees and interest must therefore be defined carefully. Where the corporate tax rates of the host and parent country are equal, the tax treatment of dividends and fees and interest in the hands of the parent company is indistinguishable. Where the corporate tax rate of the host country is lower than that of the parent country, the parent company pays the full domestic tax rate on both dividends and fees and interest, and no more; again, the tax treatment of dividends and fees and interest in the hands of the parent company is identical. Where the corporate tax rate of the host country is above that of the parent country, however, then in the case of dividends a tax is paid to the revenue authorities of the host country, and double taxation reliefs and tax credits do not relieve the parent company of the tax burden represented by the difference between the rate of corporate tax in the host country and that of its own country; the parent company is therefore exposed to an additional tax charge on the dividends from subsidiaries in that country. Where fees and interest are received, however, the subsidiary company, as stated above, pays no tax to the host government, and the parent company is thus exposed only to its domestic rate of tax. The advantage of substituting fees and interest, or dividends, thus emerges only in cases where the subsidiary company's tax rate is higher than that of the parent company.

This is of course another facet of the proposition in principle that group profits should be concentrated in the area of lowest tax liability. The substitution of subsidiary dividends by an outflow from the subsidiary to the parent of royalties, fees and interest, is of course a displacement of profits from the subsidiary to the parent.

The separate attributes of each of these two methods of payments can now be discussed.

(a) Royalties

It is usual for companies, having perfected a technological process and allowed a subsidiary company to use the latter, to make a charge for such use. This is normally done for reasons of good order rather than to obtain a business return on the process itself. Royalty fees are charged in order to obtain a return on the research and development cost expended on the elaboration of the process, and are therefore asked for primarily where the process is offered for use by companies independent of the parent company. Where the parent company and its subordinate companies use the process themselves, then the return of the research and development costs involved may be expected to arise through the sale of the product and the profits on these sales. That this is an implicit principle is well recognised in industrial and official circles, and is in itself a check to the extent to which such royalty demands may arise.

An essential precondition to royalty receipts is the technological content of the industry as a whole. Certain industries, such as chemicals, oil, electronics, have a high degree of technological input and a correspondingly high rate of innovation. Other industries, such as machinery, mining, plantations, have a lower dependence on changes in processes. The incidence of royalties will therefore differ according to the nature of the industry concerned. Within this context, much will also depend on the innovating capacity of the parent company itself. Clearly, only those parent companies producing a consistent flow of innovations will be in a position to obtain consistent payments of royalties.

This brings the discussion to the central point involved. The degree of commitment of the subsidiary to processes belonging to the parent company must be extensive if the latter is to derive a substantial income from the royalties on these. The opportunity for the parent company to raise the rate of royalty payments above the normal in order to increase these returns is limited, for the reasons explained in the previous paragraph. It should also be borne in mind that the taxation authorities of most countries exercise some vigilance in this matter, and may be expected to intervene where royalty rates appear high, on the grounds that these constitute 'concealed dividends'.

Finally it is worth recalling that royalty payments are themselves charges against incomes, and where they are substantial, conduce to a low level of profit for the subsidiary. Such a result could have adverse consequences for the subsidiary when, for instance, a need for local loan capital arises. A consistently low level of apparent profit might also have the effect of discouraging the efforts of the subsidiary's management.

(b) Management and Other Service Fees

Similar considerations to those noted above arise in the case of management and service fees. A high degree of managerial and technical expertise must be habitual to the industry concerned, and a high reservoir of such expertise must exist in the parent company concerned for this to enter into consideration as a significant factor. A variety of natural and official circumstances militate against rates of payment which deviate from the recognised norm, or which—assuming these conditions are satisfied—represent a large proportion of the earnings of the subsidiary.

(c) Conclusions on Royalties and Fees

The foregoing considerations suggest that although individual circumstances may vary widely from firm to firm and from situation to situation, the overall level of returns to parent companies under this heading is unlikely to constitute a large part of the income arising from the subsidiary company's operations.

Available data appears to bear out this general conclusion. As is shown on page 36 of Part I, total receipts by United States-based companies of royalties and fees amounted to some $5,000 m. over the period 1964–68, as compared with a total of some $24,000 m. in dividend receipts; i.e. a proportion of some 20 per cent. British receipts for the sole year in which they are recorded (1969) amounted to 4 per cent of dividend returns.

(d) Loan Interest

A heightened level of loan interest has as its precondition an augmented supply of loan capital from the parent to the subsidiary. In a number of respects such a practice would fall in with the inherent needs of a multi-company group. The parent frequently prefers to meet the new capital needs of its subordinate companies by granting loans rather than by supplying equity. In the first case the capital is lost only temporarily to the parent, since the loan must be redeemed, and in the interval interest must be paid; in the second case the parents' capital is irrecoverable, and dividends may or may not be returned, depending on the financial health of the subsidiary. When to this is added the consideration that in the international sphere the loan interest may, in certain circumstances, confer a tax benefit upon the parent, then the appeal of this alternative method of transfer of subsidiaries' resources is clear.

However, an important qualification to the above point must be made. It would be wrong to suppose that at any time after the initial period of installation of a subsidiary the parent company is in any realistic way faced with a simple choice as between providing equity capital with a putative return of dividends, and loan capital with a guaranteed return of both interest and the capital sum. As the flow of funds tables on pages 54–55 and 58–59 of Part I show, the established subsidiary is a going business concern generating profits primarily from its own internal genera- tion of funds, and secondarily, from a variety of external financing sources of which the parent company is by no means the largest. The parent com- pany, however, by reason of its ownership of all, or of the majority of the shares of the subsidiary company, is in any case the sole or major recipient of its distributed profits or dividends. Even a large increase in the parent's habitual allotment of loan capital will not, in these circumstances, greatly affect the balance between the overall dividends and loan interest paid by the subsidiary. Pari passu the supply or denial of equity capital from the parent will affect the latter's entitlements of dividends as follows: not at all in the case of 100%-owned subsidiaries; in a diminished proportion in the case of majority-held subsidiaries. Furthermore, even a large in- crease in the amount of parent's equity would, given the financing struc- ture of the typical subsidiary, have a relatively small effect on the latter's propensity to pay dividends.

Indeed, in the case of a mature multiple company group, the optimum financial structure will differ somewhat significantly from the model posed in the first paragraph above. It will be in the best interests of the group if loan capital is obtained from sources external to the group as a whole, thus sparing the financial resources both of the parent and of the subsidiaries. This is evident from the flow of funds tables on earlier pages. As regards equity capital, the parent will still be best advised to maintain its own supply at a minimum level, consistent with avoiding the need on the part of subsidiaries to obtain outside equity and so to dilute the parent's ownership.

In circumstances where the above considerations do not apply, that is to say, where the subsidiary is not well-established, and where therefore its cash flow on the one hand, and its access to external loan capital on the other, are not so large as both to make its profit prospects reliable, and its parent's capital contribution relatively modest, then the choice as between parent's equity and parent's loan capital is still not as clear as might be supposed. In a newly-founded subsidiary the parent's funds, in whatever form, will constitute a crucial and large proportion of the subsidiary's balance sheet. At the same time, it will be true to say that the prospects of dividend payments are relatively uncertain. In these circumstances the parent company's freedom of choice is far from large. Too great an emphasis on loan capital will place the subsidiary in the position where it is unable to service these charges, and where its balance sheet will be so burdened as to lessen its ability to obtain essential short-term financing locally. Thus the parent company will have little option but to supply equity capital. This indeed reflects no more than the conventional picture of industrial investment as it is commonly seen at the outset of a business project: the element of equity capital is high, and that of profit returns, low. As the project matures, the capital exposure declines, whilst its yield increases.

Thus, whilst there are no doubt transitional positions where the parent company enjoys genuine freedom of choice as between loan and share capital, with a certainty of influencing thereby the form of income accruing to it, it appears reasonable to conclude that in the general run of events the parent's option as between loan capital and equity will not significantly affect the level of dividends received by it, and that these dividends would in any case be substantially greater than the loan interest paid.

This conclusion appears to be supported by available data. In 1969 and 1970, total loan interest received by United States-based parent companies amounted to $1,034 m. Total dividend receipts amounted to $6,220 m. The dividend/loan interest ratio in this case is 6·2 to 1.[9] United Kingdom statistics show[10] that in the years 1963–70 inclusive, British-based companies received £1,152 m. in dividends from their overseas subsidiaries and associates; in the same period they received £54 m. in loan interest. The ratio of the two is thus 21·3 to 1.

(e) Transfer Price Mechanism

In the above it has been shown that parent companies can in principle divert the flow of subsidiaries' resources out of the channel of dividends, either by obtaining them in the form of non-taxable profits (i.e. loan interest) or by claiming them in the form of operating charges upon the subsidiary before a profit is struck (i.e. managerial fees and royalties).

The transfer price mechanism is an example of the latter method, and is applied to the sale of goods and services by the parent company to the subsidiary. Under this method the parent company sets such a price on these sales as substantially to enlarge its own margin of profit upon them. This will have the simultaneous effect of reducing the margin of profit of the subsidiary by an equivalent amount. The taxable earnings of the subsidiary, and its ability to pay taxable dividends to the parent company, will be proportionately reduced. At the same time, the operating

[9] *Survey of Current Business,* October 1970 and 1971. Technical note: pages 37 and 38 respectively.
[10] *Business Monitor M4,* 1971.

T.F.R.O.M.E.—D

revenues of the parent company and its own profits will be correspondingly enlarged. Thus, by an appropriate adjustment of the transfer prices, the parent company is able to 'shift' profits from the subsidiary to itself. Alternatively, of course, by paying significantly raised prices on its purchases of materials and services from the subsidiary, it can accumulate profits in the latter rather than in its own accounts.

This process is a customary and well-publicised feature of the financing of international oil companies, due primarily to the preference of host governments for large taxable revenues within their territories, and to the tacit acceptance by downstream governments of high-priced crude oil imports for reasons of overall fuel policy (see pages 21 and 22 of Part I). By synecdoche, this characteristic has been attributed to international enterprise as a whole. It will remain for consideration below whether this assumption is in all ways correct.

For the transfer price mechanism to work to the benefit of the group's finances as a whole, a number of preconditions must be satisfied. In the first place a sales flow as between the subsidiary and the parent must exist. More important, this flow of sales must be substantial enough to affect the profit outcome of the parent and the subsidiary. Clearly, intergroup transactions which represented, say, 1–2 per cent of the parent company's total purchases would have little effect on the latter's profits; and vice versa.

The act of investing abroad does not necessarily set up a flow of supplies from the parent to the subsidiary, or from the subsidiary to the parent; indeed the opposite may be the natural result of the decision. A company normally invests abroad because it has decided that rather than manufacture its product at home and export it to the market of destination, it should install manufacturing facilities in that location, and supply the market from local sources; a manufacturing arrangement tending to exclude movement of goods between the two areas has thus come into being. This observation does not, of course, apply to investment in purely distribution facilities abroad. However, as shown on page 14 of Part I, these investments form a very small proportion of the total (8 per cent for the United States; 15 per cent for the UK). The normal manufacturing investment project abroad will tend to be an image reflection, possibly in microcosm, of a parent company, having no necessary materials flow link with it. There will of course be cases where certain materials or accessories, or where certain services other than patents and managerial and technical expertise, are made available by the parent company. Indeed, a high level of interchange of parts and assemblies is known to exist in, for instance, the automotive and electronic industries. However, the above description is broadly applicable to manufacturing industry as a whole.

Statistical evidence relating to the above point is sparse, but the matter was investigated with some thoroughness in the Reddaway Report.[11] The results produced by the Reddaway Report showed purchases by a sample of British subsidiaries, representing about 71 per cent of total British investment in manufacturing and mining in the countries taken, of 'capital equipment', 'input items', and 'goods for resale' from the UK. These were expressed as follows:

	% Annual Average 1955-64
Purchases of Capital Equipment as a percentage of subsidiaries' total expenditure on fixed assets	9·5
Purchases of input items as a percentage of the total value of production of the subsidiary	3·1
Purchase of goods for resale as a percentage of total sales of goods and services by the subsidiary	5·8

It should be noticed that the above figures represent the proportionate purchases of subsidiaries from the UK as a whole. The inference to be drawn from this, however, is that subsidiaries' actual purchases from their parents, which can only be a part of their total purchases from the UK, must be very small indeed.

It appears to follow from the above that the level of trade between parents and subsidiaries will be significant only where there is a high degree of vertical integration within the group. By this is meant a situation in which substantial quantities of materials are sent from the subsidiaries to the parent, or vice versa, for further processing. The materials could in principle be either raw materials or semi-processed materials. On the whole, it appears unlikely that the parent companies of international groups, which themselves constitute the most advanced manufacturers in the industrialised countries, would be in a position to produce semi-processed products for perfecting into more sophisticated forms by their subsidiaries. The direction of flow of semi-processed materials is therefore likely, in most cases, to be from the subsidiary to the parent. As regards raw materials, the flow must, by definition, as far as Western European-based international groups are concerned, proceed from subsidiaries to parents, since Western Europe is broadly devoid of raw materials. Even in the case of North America, where raw materials abound, the point relative to degrees of sophistication mentioned above would seem to apply. It is in fact unlikely that American international parents would send raw materials to subsidiaries overseas for processing into finished products, rather than carry out the operation in their domestic plants. The foregoing consideration suggests, therefore, that the scope for high intergroup trade lies primarily in the movement of raw materials from

[11] *The Effects of UK Direct Investment Overseas*, Department of Applied Economics, University of Cambridge, 1967.

subsidiaries to their parents in Western Europe, involving such industries as mining, plantations, and oil. The model implied even by this assumption may, in the light of the Reddaway Report, be imperfect. The report found that British-owned overseas subsidiaries in the mining and plantation field were engaged in the world-wide sale of their production, rather than in the exclusive supply of their UK parent. Thus mining subsidiaries were found over the period 1955–64 to have sold only 9·5 per cent of their output to their UK parent; as regards plantations, the report dealt primarily with rubber and tea producers and stated the following: 'No sales were reported as being made directly to UK parent companies, and indeed virtually all rubber and tea is sold to unidentified buyers on the open market'.[12] Sugar-producing subsidiaries of UK parents were covered in the above figures for the manufacturing industry quoted from the report. It is possible, but presumably unlikely, that other plantations not examined in the Reddaway Report behaved differently.

The upshot of the above findings appears to be that the level of trade between subsidiaries and parents in the raw materials production field may be unevenly weighted. There is no reason to suppose that receipts of raw materials do not form a large part of the parent company's purchases; on the other hand, sales of raw materials to the parent appear to form only a small part of the subsidiaries' total sales. An adjustment of the price at which these raw materials is exchanged would therefore affect the total profits of the parent, but would have only a marginal bearing on those of the subsidiary. Of course, the residual sales of the subsidiary could go to other subsidiaries of the parent established in industrialised areas, and also engaged in the manufacture of finished products. In this case, a concerted arrangement on prices as between the parent and all the subsidiaries could result in a true shift of profits to or from the raw material producing side of the business. However, the wording of the Reddaway Report does not indicate that such other finished producers exist within the group, and the nature of the mining market suggests that the same may be true for that sector. In the case of oil, of course, the normal pattern is for the total output of crude oil by the upstream companies to be sold to refining and distribution subsidiaries of the same group downstream. The level of vertical integration and therefore of trade within the group is very high.

It follows, therefore, from all of the foregoing, that the physical basis for the use of the transfer price mechanism, i.e. a high level of trade between members of the group, may not be present to a large degree, at least in most industries.[13]

[12] *The Effects of UK Direct Investment Overseas*, Department of Applied Economics, University of Cambridge, 1967/68, Chapter 7, Appendix I.
[13] This should not be taken to contravert the findings by a number of bodies, in particular by the United States Department of Commerce, that exports from the US are directed in large degree (some 30 per cent of the total) to the subsidiaries overseas of American

The above findings must be considered in relation to the third and final general point. This is the ultimate effect on the group's taxation as a result of the shifting of profits between members. As was stated, profits may be accumulated either in the accounts of the parent or in those of the producing subsidiary. If they are accumulated in the accounts of the parent, then a tax alleviation will arise only where the corporate tax rate of the subsidiary is above that of the parent, and where the latter would suffer a residual burden of double taxation if the profits were transmitted to the parent from the subsidiary in the form of dividends. Where the tax levels of the subsidiary are either below or the same as those of the parent, no advantage arises from shifting profits. Per contra, shifting of profits into the accounts of the producing subsidiary may, if the relative corporate tax levels are appropriate, lead to a higher accumulation of profit on the transaction in the subsidiary than would have been achieved in the parent company. On the other hand, this does nothing to direct group profits into the hands of the parent company, which is by definition the central object of any multi-company group, as observed above. Accumulation of profit in the hands of the subsidiary is in fact equivalent to the 'nil dividend remittance' case examined above (page 91). This operation is of interest to the parent company primarily as a means of financing the creation of new fixed assets. Beyond this, there is no significant financial advantage, and, indeed, potential disadvantages arise. In the case of the oil industries, again, there is in fact a substantial requirement for new fixed assets in the producer-countries. The same may not necessarily be true for the mining and plantation sector.

The conclusion to all of the foregoing therefore seems to be that the physical basis in terms of trade levels, for transfer price techniques, is limited, and that where this exists, the usefulness of such techniques will depend on a careful evaluation of the balance between relative taxation burdens, financing needs, and official requirements.

More detailed considerations

The detailed considerations which follow are based partly on the difficulties and advantages found by national companies, and partly on those found by international companies.

Apart from the general position outlined above, a number of other matters, of a more detailed and practical nature, affect the working of a transfer pricing system. These are enumerated and commented upon briefly below.

companies. The measures in each case are different. The Reddaway Report calculates receipts from UK parents as a proportion of total receipts by the subsidiary from all sources—this is the measure required for present purposes. The proportion involved may be small. The US Department of Commerce measures total despatches from all parents to their subsidiaries as a proportion of total exports of the country of the parent. This proportion may be large.

It is perhaps worth remarking at the outset that the transfer pricing system is an appurtenance not so much of international companies, but of the multi-company groups as such. It is a technique applicable to any company group having an internal circulation of goods and services, whether this group is based nationally or internationally. Transfer pricing techniques have long been the subject of study, and indeed of practice, of company groups within national boundaries. This has given rise to little comment in the past—perhaps understandably so. Within the national context, these are matters reasonably held to be within the internal purview of the company itself. It should perhaps be stressed that the techniques do not raise issues of ethics or of business integrity. It is for a firm so to order the pricing of material movements within its framework as to conduce to the greatest commercial efficiency of the business as a whole. The sole test is the scale of the profits which the parent company is ultimately able to distribute to its shareholders. If transfer pricing has evoked comment in the sphere of international companies, this is because it has the effect of moving profits from one segment of the international company to another, i.e. from one country to another. Such objections therefore as have been raised to transfer pricing by international companies are, albeit strong, wholly political; the issues in international, as in national, business are those neither of ethics nor of business equity.

Administrative

In some, if not most, industrial sectors, particularly perhaps in engineering, the flow of material between parents and subsidiaries, however small in relative terms, may comprise many hundreds of products and product variations. A coherent system of price management, so as to affect earnings in all parts of the group at any opportune moment, would have to be extremely complex. It is probable that the size and cost of the administrative apparatus necessary for this would outweigh the financial benefits resulting from profit shifting.

Efficiency

An inter-group pricing system designed to transfer profits from one sector to another will necessarily develop prices which in many cases will bear no relation to the value of the products either on a market or production cost assessment. The competitive efficiency with which the goods are produced would thus be obscured from the view of the group's central management. Similarly, the very operation of arbitrary displacement of profit from one company to another obscures judgement of the true return on capital in any one company. It is perhaps worth noting that a recent study in the UK,[14] based on the survey of the practice of some

[14] *Transfer Pricing; The Measure of Management Performance in Multi-Divisional Companies*, British Institute of Management, Management Survey Report No. 8, 1971.

300 major British companies, found that the companies concerned in all cases based their inter-unit prices either upon costs of production or upon the going market price; in no case did the fixing of prices appear to be actuated solely by the motive of profit-shifting.

Morale

The essential principle of the multi-company group is the co-ordination of the work of legally separate identities, each with its own structure of management, control, and finance. The tendency for constituent companies to acquire a marked identity, and indeed esprit de corps, of their own is inevitable; this is particularly true of those members of international groups where central management policy has been in favour of appointing nationals to positions of executive authority. Conflict can arise where, in face of this trend, individual companies are required by central group management to run a continuous operating loss for the financial advantage of another member of the group.

Minority Shareholders

Where sustained low profits or a loss are sought in a subsidiary company, a part of the equity of which is held by outside shareholders, a demand for the maintenance of existing dividend levels could arise. This is particularly likely where the minority participation is in the hands of a single shareholder—possibly another company. In these circumstances the possibilities of transfer pricing are limited.

Auditors

All component companies, by reason of their separate legal character, are required to submit their company accounts to scrutiny by impartial auditors. The latter are professionally bound to note a decline in profit levels for comparable products, particularly where this is abrupt, and where it is not explicable in normal commercial terms. Whilst such auditors, reports may have little significance for the parent company where the latter is the sole owner, it may have some impact where there is a minority holding and where this is widely dispersed. In the case of 100 per cent ownership by the parent, the auditors' report may also come to the notice of the fiscal and other authorities of the host country.

Fiscal Implications

Declining or disappearing profit margins necessarily reduce the revenue accruing through corporate taxation to the government of the company concerned. The governments of a number of countries do not look upon such developments with favour, particularly when it is believed that the absent profits are being transferred to another country. A number, in fact, have given their fiscal authorities powers to intervene. In the United

States, for example, the Internal Revenue Service has authority to reallocate income among members of a corporate group.[15] The United Kingdom Inland Revenue has similar powers.

Customs Implications

Where the price of goods exchanged between group members across international frontiers is altered, the duty payable on those goods in the country of receipt will also vary, since the duty is normally assessed ad valorem or is otherwise related to the invoiced value of the merchandise. Where the transfer price is increased, the duty payable by the recipient company will also increase; this will serve further to diminish the profits of the recipient company as a result of the price change. The extra costs, where the parent company is concerned, may indeed be so great as to vitiate the advantages of the whole operation. On the other hand, where the price change is downwards, then the customs revenue arising in the recipient country will be curtailed. Here again, the governments of many countries are vigilant to ensure that their revenues are not debilitated by non-commercial price movements in the transactions of internationally connected corporate bodies. The customs authorities of most countries have in fact the right to raise the invoice valuation for duty assessment purposes where it appears to them that this is understated. In addition, local industrial interests may be affected, particularly where, as is often the case, the reduced price is intended to allow the recipient company to reduce the cost of its sales to the market. Allegations of dumping may well arise, with injurious results to the group. The Canadian customs authorities have the power to apply anti-dumping duties to imports as soon as it is established that the invoice price is lower than that normally practiced in the home market of the exporter, and without considering whether such low-priced imports are in fact causing damage in the Canadian market; these duties are then held in escrow until the Canadian Tariff Board has reached a conclusion as to whether damage has been sustained. Short of the application of anti-dumping duty, undesirable results can emerge: for example, the United States customs authorities are empowered, on the establishment of a prima facie case of dumping, to suspend duty assessment pending the determination of the case and the imposition of a dumping duty. Since the duty exposure of the goods in question from that point onwards becomes unknown, the practical effect is invariably to terminate imports. All customs authorities, during the investigation of dumping and other allegations, have extensive powers of search and examination in company books and accounts.

[15] Section 482 of the US Revenue Code states: '. . . the Secretary . . . may distribute, apportion, or allocate gross income, deductions, credits, or allowances . . . if he determines that such distribution, appointment, or allocation is necessary in order to prevent evasion of taxes or clearly to reflect the income of any such organisations, trades or businesses'.

Exchange Control

The prices at which goods are exported or imported from or into any given country necessarily influence the balance of payments of that country. Transfer pricing arrangements can therefore also come within the surveillance of the Exchange Control authorities. In the case, for instance, of the United Kingdom, the Exchange Control Act[16] states that: 'The exportation of goods . . . is hereby prohibited except with the permission of the Treasury, unless the Commissioners of Customs & Excise are satisfied that the amount of the payment that has been made or is to be made is such as to represent a return for the goods which is in all the circumstances satisfactory in the national interest.'

(v) *International Base Companies*

As earlier stated, it is open to international companies, in face of a possible double taxation burden on dividends paid by a subsidiary to the parent, to route these payments through an international base company where tax conditions may be more favourable. It will be apparent that where the corporate tax rate on the subsidiary is less than that of the parent company, and where the tax rate applicable to dividends received by a financial subsidiary in another country is less than both, it can be of advantage to direct the dividends to the latter location. For example, parent companies corporate tax rates may be at 50 per cent, whilst that of the subsidiary may be 35 per cent. If an international financial subsidiary is set up in a country where the tax on such dividend receipts is only 5 per cent, it will be to the advantage of the group if the subsidiary taxed at 35 per cent were to transfer dividends to the international financial company.

The merit of this operation does not lie in the immediate effect of this transfer. Funds lodged with the international base company are, necessarily, not funds in the hands of the parent company, the only quarter where the group's profits can be effectively accumulated and distributed to shareholders. As soon as the subsidiary's dividends reach the parent company, whether direct or via the international financial company, the full tax rate of 50 per cent will have to be paid, and the tax is not in any long-term sense avoided.

The true merit of the interposing of an international base company lies in the assistance the latter can give to current financial operations within the group during the time in which it holds the parent company's funds. It may, from the larger reservoir of capital which it will hold, make loans to the operating subsidiary in question, or issue new equity capital, or it may of course provide funds of this sort to other subsidiaries of the parent company in other countries. As an example of the first operation,

[16] Exchange Control Act, Part 4, Section 23, Sub-section 1 (b).

T.F.R.O.M.E.—D*

on the supposition that the subsidiary company's tax rate was 35 per cent, the parent company's 50 per cent, and the international financial subsidiary's tax 5 per cent, and that £100 of dividends from the operating subsidiary would amount to £50 in the hands of the parent, and to $£100 - 35 - \left(\dfrac{5 \times 65}{100}\right)$, or £61·75 in the hands of the base company: the financial subsidiary would thus have an additional £11·75 to lend or to contribute as equity. The avoidance for the parent company of a loss of this order (viz. 11·75 per cent of available dividend, and 23 per cent of the subsequent provision of capital) through the mere passage of the money across national frontiers, is important; particularly where exchange control arrangements in the parent company may be such as to render the subsequent outflow of capital difficult.

It is in contemplation of the tax and exchange control issues outlined above that most parent companies perhaps consider the greater utility of the international parent company as lying in the second of the two operations mentioned above, i.e. in the distribution to other subsidiaries of funds arising from any one subsidiary. The operations of an international company group consist not merely in the passage of capital from the parent, and of dividends from the separate subsidiaries back to the parent; at its optimum, it will include a degree of movement of available funds from one subsidiary to another. It may well occur that a subsidiary, by reason of the success of its operations in one country, may be enjoying a high level of profits. At the same time, a subsidiary in another country may be embarking upon a new capital investment project, or may be encountering a period of transient financial deficit. The surplus resources of the one company can be used to replenish those of the other. In a typical group, simultaneous situations of this sort will be present in different parts of the total network at any given time, and will recur continuously. This state of affairs is typical not of the international company group, but of the multi-company group as such. What is required for the proper co-ordination and deployment of internally generated resources of this kind is a central clearing house, or treasury. Where the multi-company group is concentrated within the boundaries of a single national state, the function of central fund assembly and dispersal is of course undertaken by the parent company. This essential link is, however, in the case of the international company group, broken by the interposition of national frontiers and the varying tax rates and exchange control restrictions which these bring with them. The parent company of the international group is effectively debarred from exercising its proper function as the central reservoir of the group's finances. It would not, in these circumstances, be sufficient for the parent company simply to direct its international subsidiaries to transmit funds to and fro between themselves as the need arose. The supply and demand for funds does not coincide exactly in time, and a point of central collection and retention is required; more importantly, the rules of company law in all countries, and those of exchange control in many, are such that a subsidiary is not legally able to supply money direct to another subsidiary. Dividends can only be paid to the shareholder; the provision of loans is subject to certain limitations of company law, and to others, more specific, of exchange control. The provision of equity capital makes the supplier a shareholder of the recipient country—an outcome certainly not desired within the multi-company group as a whole. Clearly, where the parent company is effectively incapacitated, a substitute central reservoir is required.

This substitute role is excellently provided by the international base company. Being located in a country of low taxation and moderate, or non-existent, exchange controls, it is able with the least impediment to attend to the amassing and dissemination of central group funds. Being the sole or major shareholder of the various subsidiaries, it does not encounter the bars to the movement of capital or dividends mentioned above. Being itself wholly-owned by the parent company, it is in a position to transfer at regular intervals the group profits it has accumulated to the parent company for distribution to the final shareholders of the international group as a whole.

It was mentioned above that the international base company first comes into use where a given subsidiary's tax rate is lower than that of the parent. Clearly, where the rate is equal to or higher than that of the parent, then the cumulative tax payable both by the parent and the base company is the same, and there is no advantage, on tax grounds, of re-routeing the payment. Where, in fact, the general level of taxation among the subsidiaries is equal to or higher than that of the parent, then there is no advantage in establishing a base company—the exchange control considerations apart. The foregoing applies, of course, where normal double taxation agreements and tax credit arrangements are in force, and economic double taxation as such does not occur. An international base company is always of use in those cases where the parent company is situated in a country without the above procedures, and where economic double taxation, in the full sense of the word, applies to its receipts of dividends from subsidiaries elsewhere.

All international base companies of any significance are established, it should be added, with the knowledge and consent of the fiscal and exchange control authorities of all the countries affected; i.e. of those of the parent company, the operating subsidiary, and the international base company. That this should be so is perhaps to be expected. The fiscal and exchange control arrangements of the country of the operating subsidiary are unaffected by the direction in which the dividends flow when they are remitted outside that country; it is immaterial whether they go to the country of the parent or the country of the base company.

The due taxes deductible from the operating company's profits are fully collected in both cases; the normal operation of exchange control is not affected. As regards the authorities of the base company: the taxes collected on the dividend receipts are, albeit low, those duly prescribed by the government of that country; exchange control barriers are small, where not non-existent, as explained above. As regards the authorities of the parent company, the profits collected by the base company are, as explained above, necessarily transferred in full in due course to the parent country. Indeed, it follows from the foregoing that the profits eventually transferred to the parent country are greater than those which would have materialised, had the original dividends from the operating subsidiaries been remitted immediately and direct to the parent country. The central purpose of the interposition of the base company is to use the group's earnings to transact further profitable undertakings before these earnings, and the additional profits so made, are transmitted for submission to the tax claim of the parent country. If the purpose of the creation of the base company is therefore successfully achieved, then the ultimate profits repatriated to the parent country, and the tax revenue obtained from them by the fiscal authorities of that country, will be greater than if the base company had not existed. The same principle applies to the foreign exchange position of the parent country. In relation to an identical original capital export by the parent company, a larger dividend return will materialise in the case of the existence of an international base company than where the individual subsidiaries remit their dividends direct, and immediately, to the parent company. All of the foregoing is true where the country of the parent company is able to accept a postponement of repatriations for a reasonable period. Where either the revenue or the balance of payments circumstances of the parent country are such that repatriations are urgently needed, then there is less scope for the useful operation of an international base company.

In all of these operations there can, it seems evident, be no imputation of loss of tax revenue or of foreign exchange. The position of the country of the operating subsidiary is, as shown above, unchanged, and that of the parent country will be improved provided the latter can wait for these benefits. The only tax foregone is the corporate tax of the base company's country, but this is so by the deliberate choice of the government of that country, made no doubt to encourage the establishment on its territory of profitable international operations which would not otherwise take place there. It is of course for the same reason that parent companies in other countries take advantage of these conditions.

CHAPTER 6

Exchange Considerations

As stated in the introduction to Part II, the international company is in essence no more than a multi-company group, the component members of which are situated in different countries.

The effect of this is that the financial flows of this particular kind of multi-company group are conducted not in one currency, but in many different currencies. This constitutes a further major complexity confronting the financial managers of an international company. The number of currencies involved may be very large—some international companies operate in as many as twenty or thirty individual countries—and the transactions involved will be varied: comprising, as shown above, movements of share and loan capital from the parent to the subsidiaries; of dividend, capital and interest payments, and royalty and fee payments from the subsidiaries to the parent; of some loan and fee transactions between subsidiaries; and of the same mixture of transactions between the subsidiaries and a financial base company, and between the latter and the parent company. Where external finances for the group as a whole are sought in the international market, then yet a further currency may come into play.

Use of a multiplicity of currencies is a complicating factor if only because of the variety of values involved, and of conversion operations required. Consolidation of the balance sheets of the group, and exact appraisal of the assets and performance of the group and its component companies, requires sizeable and repeated recalculations which do not arise in the case of multi-company groups operating within the boundaries of single states.

However, the major complication lies in the possibility of changes in the relative values of the currencies concerned. The magnitude of this risk can be gauged from the fact that between 1948 and 1965 there were fifty changes in par values in 31 different countries.[1]

The aforementioned administrative disadvantages of operations in multiple currencies are in the nature of inconveniences rather than basic

[1] J. Keith Horsefield, *The International Monetary Fund 1945-1965*, Washington, D.C. 1969. Volume II, pages 116 *et seq.*

obstacles to the normal functioning of the group. On the other hand, changes in the relative values of the currencies used can have a far-reaching impact on the central finances of the company, and the latter will accordingly be considered more closely in the following.

(a) EFFECT ON INTERNATIONAL COMPANIES OF CHANGES IN PAR VALUES

The effects of a change in the par value of a currency, or in that currency's devaluation or revaluation, is to alter the value of all property in that country, whether physical or financial, in the terms of the currencies of other countries; ergo: a house worth £1,000 in the United Kingdom at one rate of exchange may be worth $2,800 in terms of United States currency. A United States citizen who was the possessor of the house would consider this property as being the equivalent to him of that sum of us dollars. If the pound is devalued by 14·3 per cent in terms of the us dollar, then £1,000 becomes equal to $2,400, and the United States citizen who is the owner of the house in question has suffered a loss of $400. Similarly, a rent of £100 per annum paid by a tenant of the house to the United States owner would fall from a dollar value of $280 to $240. In the case of an equivalent revaluation of the pound, the United States owner would have equivalent gains. Where the United States citizen had liabilities in pounds —for example, in the form of a loan upon the house—then devaluation of the pound would clearly reduce the number of dollars required for the repayment of capital interest, and revaluation of the pound would increase the number of dollars required.

(i) Primacy of the Impact on the Parent Company

Proceeding from the above simple illustration, it is possible to analyse the effects of currency changes upon the financing of international companies. It will first be apparent from the example that a parity change does not affect the citizen of the country concerned; only those whose financial assets and liabilities in the country concerned must be valued in the form of other currencies can be affected. In the case of international companies, the subsidiary resident in the country of devaluation or revaluation is unaffected in its internal finances. However, those other members of the group from whom it receives, or to whom it sends capital and income, are affected. Since the subsidiary is a member of a multi-company group, it follows by definition that a subsidiary's dividends will go only to the parent company. Similarly the subsidiary's capital from within the group will come wholly or mainly from the parent. Thus in the case of exchange risk considerations—as in all else in the financing of multinational companies—the effect on the parent is the primary consideration. This point perhaps deserves fuller clarification.

Income

A situation could be envisaged in which the currency of the subsidiary company was devalued *vis-à-vis* that of the parent company, but where the same change did not take place in the currency of another subsidiary in another country, i.e. where both subsidiaries, in countries (A) and (B), experienced the same devaluation *vis-à-vis* country (C) of the parent. In this case, by diverting a major part of its trade to the subsidiary in country (B), and by suitably organising its prices, subsidiary (A) could effectively transfer its profit to subsidiary (B). This profit would then not go in the form of dividends from country (A) to the parent in country (C), and the devaluation loss would not be sustained.

There are, of course, practical considerations involved in the above proposition, as has been mentioned earlier. It is necessary for the requisite level of inter-trade between the companies to be present, and it must also be possible, in the light of the production and sales position of the companies, for the switch in trade to be carried out. Above all a suitable transfer price mechanism has to be installed, and a number of difficulties arise in this respect, as suggested earlier.

However, the primary point affecting the proposition is, of course, that the profits, once shifted to subsidiary (B), are still of no avail to the multi-company group as a whole. These profits do not benefit the central finances of the group until they have been placed in the possession of the parent company. Since country (B) devalued equally with country (A), the exchange loss on the dividends will be postponed—but none the less incurred when the profits are finally transmitted to the parent.

Other variants which might be conceived appear to lead to similar conclusions. Where no other subsidiary experiences a devaluation similar to that of country (A), then clearly no case for transfer of profits arises. The only other case which may be envisaged is that where another subsidiary e.g., the subsidiary in country (B), experiences a revaluation which will bring its par value above that of the parent in country (C). The transfer of accumulated profits from country (B) to country (C) will clearly entail an advantage to the parent. However, this will be offset by the equivalent loss on the profits passed on the devalued subsidiary (A) to the revalued subsidiary (B). Thus in the case of the devaluation of the currency of a given subsidiary, there appears to be no means by which the ultimate exchange loss upon the dividends accruing to the parent may be avoided.

In the opposite contingency—that of a revaluation of country (A)—then of course the parent company enjoys a gain in the dividends transmitted to it. As against this, however, the cost to the parent of capital contributed by it to the subsidiary will be raised. None the less, as was shown in Part I, outflows of parent capital normally fall below inflows of subsidiaries' dividends, and it can therefore be said that as a general rule revaluation in a subsidiary's country is of benefit to the parent.

Capital

This leads on to a consideration of the effect of parity changes on capital movements within international multi-company groups. The direct relationship between parent and subsidiary has already been described. It is not, however, uncommon for loan capital (as described earlier) to be passed between subsidiaries of the same group. If one subsidiary, paying loan capital and interest to another subsidiary, is subject to a currency revaluation, it will benefit. The subsidiary, it may be felt, will then generate a higher profit, which will be transmitted in terms of greater dividends to the parent. If, of course, the loan is denominated in its own currency, then it will be the second subsidiary which achieves higher profit ratings, and consequently higher dividend remittances to the parent. These considerations leave out of account the added tax liability arising from higher loan interest income and higher profit remittances to the parent; it is unlikely, though, that this will entirely outweigh the reverse gain. More important, the above analysis has ignored the fact that the cost of supplying future group capital to the revalued subsidiary will be increased—thus offsetting the gain on the repayment of the existing loan. Higher cost loans to the subsidiary will result in an eventual loss to the parent, either directly, or through the reduced profitability of other group members supplying the capital. Again then, the general rule of the primacy of the impact of parity changes on the parent company appears to be confirmed.

The International Base Company

The position of the group where an international base company is used must now be considered. There is the evident first possibility that the currency of the country of the international base company may be changed in value. If the change is upwards against that of the parent company, then the group income arising to the parent company is increased. However, the case is an exact parallel to that examined above in relation to a possible transfer of profits as between subsidiaries (*A*) and (*B*), since the parent's gain in its dividends from the international base company will be offset by the latter's loss in the value of dividends received from other subsidiaries in the group. Equivalent and opposite effects would flow from a devaluation of the currency of the international base company. In short, fluctuations upwards or downwards in the value of that company's currency would be offset by equivalent and opposite effects on its receipts of income from the remaining subsidiaries of the group whose currencies moved with or against it. The net position is that only where all the subsidiaries' currencies moved either upwards or downwards in exact accordance with the change in the international base company's currency could there be a resultant effect on the parent company. In short, the role of the international base company, in foreign exchange matters, appears to be neutral.

This does not, of course, prevent this company from so organising the streams of capital and income within the group, as to defer or indeed to mitigate the ultimate effect upon the parent company, much as it does in the field of taxation. Where, for instance, devaluation may be threatened in the country of one subsidiary, it may be possible for the international base company to have recourse to dividends from that country in the first instance, rather than from a country whose currency may be revalued; and so to assemble the group's liquid assets in a way least subject to exchange risks. Similarly, the international base company may arrange for provision of short- and long-term capital loans from subsidiaries whose currency parities may move downwards rather than upwards. These and other possible procedures will be discussed more fully below. Since in this field— unlike that of taxation—the parent company's freedom of action is equal to that of the international base company, the discussion will assume that the parent company is taking the action.

Background Economic Effects

The foregoing has examined the impact of parity changes on the parent, solely in the context of changes in the values of intra-group fund movements. Although the above embodies the essential scope of the present study, there may be some merit in considering briefly the background of general economic effects resulting from parity changes. The general economic effects of parity changes in the country of the subsidiary may perhaps alter the commercial viability of the subsidiary, and thence the level of its profit returns to the parent. Thus it might be felt that devaluation could change the terms of trade to the subsidiary's disadvantage, and so lessen its trading profitability. Alternatively, an increased level of economic inflation or deflation attendant upon the parity change might affect the subsidiary's viability. However, it must be recognised that the true nature of these developments is still a matter of economic surmise rather than of established fact. Economic observers have seen trading advantages both in devaluation and revaluation; similarly, inflationary and deflationary pressures have been ascribed both to devaluation and revaluation. In face of the conflict of view on the subject, it might best be supposed that the effect on a subsidiary's profits of general economic changes attendant on parity alterations may be neutral.

External Financing

To complete the picture it is worth considering the effect of parity changes on the group through the medium of the group's external financing. Where this is done by subsidiaries in their local currency, the foregoing comments apply. The subsidiaries' own profitability is not affected, and therefore the flow of profits to the group as a whole does not change. Where the subsidiary borrows outside the group and in another country—possibly in the international market—then a change in parities affecting the loan will increase or diminish the subsidiary's profitability, and thence the profitability of the group as a whole. Cases of subsidiaries borrowing in foreign and international markets are, however, rare. Where the parent borrows in foreign and international markets outside the group, then parity changes are reflected directly in the group's finances.

(ii) *Nature of the Impact on the Parent Company*

Having identified the parent company as the party primarily interested in parity changes affecting members of the group, it is now necessary to determine in what precise ways these effects are felt by the parent.

As demonstrated at the beginning of the present section, the basic effect of parity changes is to alter, in terms of the currency of the parent country, the value of physical and financial property, and of the income arising from it, in the subsidiary's country. This means, in brief, that the assets and liabilities of the parent company in the subsidiary company will be changed in value; further, flows of funds within international groups representing the transfer of these assets and liabilities, or of the income arising from the assets, will be subject to losses or gains resulting from changes in the parities at which the parent's currency can be converted into that of the subsidiary, and vice versa. Finally, although this is not strictly intrinsic to the financial organisation of a company, the proceeds of current trade, where this exists, will be changed in amount. The detailed nature of these effects can now be examined. For the sake of simplification, the case of devaluation of the subsidiary's currency—the least welcome of the two possibilities—will be primarily considered. Following the above line of reasoning, this examination will consider first, assets and liabilities—in the balance sheet items—and secondly, the movement of funds. It will come to broad conclusions as to whether each item lends itself to palliative action by the group.

Fixed Assets

Where a subsidiary's currency is devalued, then it follows from the foregoing that the parent should, ideally, substitute liabilities for all its assets in that country. Drawing upon the simple numerical example quoted above, the United States resident owner of a house in the UK should sell that house prior to devaluation (receiving $2,800) and purchase another house of the same sterling value of £1,000 after devaluation (at a dollar cost of $2,400). Alternatively, the house could be mortgaged in sterling, entailing, after devaluation, capital and interest repayments at a lower dollar cost. This would be drastic action on the part of a private property owner; in the case of an industrial or commercial company it is clearly impossible. A large manufacturing complex in the UK, necessarily unique in its nature, could not be the subject of a pre-emptive sale. Similarly, conversion of a subsidiary's capital to 100 per cent debt basis is excluded. The conclusion which follows from the above observation is the fundamental one held by all international financial managers in face of devaluation risks. Nothing can be done to screen fixed assets held in foreign countries from the effects of devaluation of those countries' currencies. The plant, machinery and buildings constituting those assets cannot be disposed of; they have been installed for the purpose of carrying on business, and if the objects of the group are to be attained, this business must necessarily continue. Neither can they be shielded to any major extent by countervailing long-term liabilities; the debt equity ratio of the subsidiary cannot be distorted even where putative lenders are in being; in any case, the public authorities of the subsidiary's country might well resist such large-scale funding. Moreover, there is considerable doubt whether the capital market of the country concerned would, in most cases, be of large enough capacity to absorb borrowing on the scale which might be implied. Of course, in theory the parent company could raise a currency hedge against the fixed asset value: that is to say the parent could sell, for instance, sterling forward to the amount of the assets. On the due date, assuming devaluation had intervened, the sterling could be repurchased at a lower cost in foreign currency, and a gain equivalent to the foreign currency loss on the UK fixed assets could be secured. Indeed, such a hedge could be maintained in position for some time pending an expected devaluation, at the cost of the loss on the margin between buying and selling rates. However, it is unlikely that such an operation could cover the whole value of existing assets, unless the latter were very small. Parents could nevertheless hedge on new inputs of capital. In the case of the UK, however, as of many other countries, exchange controls would require the operation of the hedge on non-resident account, a fact which would limit, if not exclude, its use.

Thus the first effect of devaluation may be said to be a reduction of the subsidiary's fixed asset value in the books of the parent company. This may affect the overall profitability of the group as a whole. However, this value will not remain static. Where inflation is in progress in the devaluing country—a not unusual circumstance—the asset value will, over the course of relatively few years, recover in the parent's books. More important, if the subsidiary conducts its business with success and profit, its asset value will continue to grow. None the less, a once-for-all loss will be incurred as a consequence of devaluation, and this cannot in principle at any time be made good.

Long-Term Liabilities

As already remarked, the parent can consider an increase in its long-term liabilities in the country concerned. This will mean, of course, either an increase in the subsidiary's long-term liabilities outside the group in its own country, or an increase in the long-term liabilities of the parent to the subsidiary. The subsidiary's opportunities for external fixed-interest financing in its home capital market are, as already stated above, limited. As regards the parent's long-term liabilities to the subsidiary: these do not in practice arise. The flow of long-term finance is from the parent to the subsidiary, for obvious practical reasons, and not in the reverse direction.

Short-Term Balance Sheet Items

In the domain of the short-term balance sheet items, devaluation presents a risk of book value loss in such items as stocks and work in progress which the parent is not in a position easily to influence. These assets must remain intact if the business is to continue. Limited opportunities for currency hedging may arise. On the other hand, truly liquid assets—cash in hand, deposits at bank, short-term investment paper, etc.—certainly provide apparent scope for pre-emptive reduction; this will be pursued in more detail below. On the liability side, there is again a possibility of enlargement of the items for accounts payable and bank credit. Outstanding intergroup trade credit can also be modified. Any trade credit extended to the subsidiary will, after devaluation, prove costly to the parent. These points will also be examined more fully below.

Flows of Funds

The exchange cost of share capital, as well as loan capital contributions from the parent, will be lower after devaluation than before. Any large contributions immediately prior to devaluation will accordingly impose an effective and substantial loss on the parent.

As stated above, contributions of long-term capital from the subsidiary to the parent do not occur; on the other hand, repayments of loan capital take place, and these will be of lower value to the parent after devaluation. In the short-term field, payments of dividends and other income will necessarily be diminished in the parent company's currency, following devaluation. Goods sold by the parent to the subsidiary will produce lower receipts after devaluation than before.

The above itemises the main areas of danger for the parent in the event of an impending downward currency movement in a subsidiary's country. The feasibility and consequences of action on these items will be examined below. Meanwhile a number of general observations appear relevant.

(iii) *General Aspects of the Effects of Changes in Par Values*
Importance of the Subsidiary's Financial Structure

A major point for notice lies in the manner in which the initial proposition, set out at the beginning of the present section, comes into play in practice. It was pointed out that a change in currency value does not affect the finances of the resident of the country of change, but becomes operative as soon as transactions occur between such a resident and a resident of another country. This principle has been broadly illuminated in the foregoing text. The essential components of the subsidiary's business—its fixed assets and long-term liabilities—as has been seen remain broadly beyond the compass of currency issues. On the other hand, short-term assets and liabilities have been seen to be more closely involved. For transfers of funds —capital contributions and repayments, dividend and interest payments, etc.—the effect of currency changes has been seen to be sharply recognisable.

However, it would be inadvisable to assume that a sharp distinction between the two categories is maintained in practice. Fund flows are themselves—as already mentioned—a derivative of balance sheet items, i.e. they are transfers of assets and liabilities, or payments of income on these. Thus an alteration in fund flows made for the purpose of accommodating a currency change cannot be without an effect on the balance sheet items. Indeed, there is a complementarity between the two; in many cases a change in a fund flow cannot be initiated without an appropriate preliminary redeployment of the balance sheet items. The more flexible the asset or liability, the more volatile may be the resultant fund flow. Hence, as remarked above, short-term assets and liabilities find themselves in closer proximity to the currency arena than long-term items, and their corresponding fund movements can be speedier.

The more important point arising from the above is, however, that pre-emptive income and other adjustments are closely interdependent with the financial structure of the company concerned. Remittances of dividends from the subsidiary to the parent could be expedited prior to devaluation; however, the feasibility of this precaution will depend to a large extent on the former's ability to increase its short-term liabilities in the form of local trade creditors and bank credit. Similarly, a suitable reduction of the parent's capital transfers in anticipation of devaluation will be contingent on the subsidiary's borrowing potential in the local fixed interest market, or in the local banking system. A reversal of trade credit in favour of the parent will again be a function of the subsidiary's liquid position, which will already be under pressure from the two directions just enumerated. All of these fund movements, both the reduction of long-term capital inputs and the conversion of short-term assets into a local bank credit/dividend outflow stream, will depend on the level of the internally-generated funds of the subsidiary. It follows from this that the various recourses enumerated are practicable only in the event of the existence of an appropriate financial structure in the subsidiary.

Long-Term Impact of Parity Changes

Secondly, the extent to which parity change consequences are ineluctable should be recognised. It has already been shown that fixed assets cannot effectively be shielded from these effects. The same is true for a number of short-term assets. Where, either in the case of balance sheet or of flow items, protective action is possible within a limited time scale, it does not avert the full eventual consequences of the parity change. Thus an acceleration of income remittances to the parent prior to devaluation may relieve the parent of devaluation losses on the current year, and may possibly forestall income remittances due for the next year, or even thereafter; but once the saving procured by this resort is exhausted, then the yearly income receipts of the parent will be permanently diminished by the devaluation margin. Similarly, losses on capital transfers to the subsidiary may be avoided in the year of devaluation, and possibly for a time thereafter; none the less, if the subsidiary is to continue in business, and indeed expand, further injections of capital from the parent are ultimately inevitable, and these will be made at the higher cost implied by the devaluation of the subsidiary's currency.

In the same way, a temporary higher debt/equity ratio in the subsidiary must be restored; hedges must be removed and further capital contributions made at the new parity; the deferment of accounts payable must be ended; bank credit must be repaid, and trade credit to the parent must be recovered. The financing structure of the subsidiary will revert to the pre-devaluation mould; the original flows, and short-and long-term assets, will revert to their previous scale, but at the lower devaluation margin implicit for the parent. Thus at the end of the process a book loss on the subsidiary's assets, both fixed- and short-term, equivalent to the devaluation margin, will have been sustained; and losses on fund movements, both as regards capital flows from the parent and income returns from the subsidiary, will have come into being.

Predictability of Parity Changes

As a background to these actions, there remains, it must be recalled, a continuous uncertainty as to whether the change in parity anticipated will in fact take place. Devaluations and revaluations, as recent history has shown, are essentially political acts arrived at in circumstances frequently prohibiting exact prediction.

Governmental decisions on changes in parities are made in circumstances both of some complexity and of some secrecy. The range of factors under consideration will be large, and will certainly exceed the economic issues immediately apparent. Thus governmental discussions will be concerned not only with the balance of trade and levels of home prices in its own country, but will include the estimated effect of a par value change on its trading partners, the level of its currency reserves, its borrowing facilities with the IMF, the Group of Ten and foreign central banks, and the conditions on which such loans might be granted. The government concerned will also take thought for any commitments regarding parity changes it may have undertaken *vis-à-vis* foreign governments and international organisations, and for the political impact of a currency change on its relations with other governments. Many if not most of these factors will remain outside the purview of the observer in the ordinary commercial field, and governmental deliberations on them will necessarily be held in private. The likelihood of the occurrence of a parity change, together with its timing and extent, are thus subjects the prediction of which present great difficulty to the lay observer.

This is borne out in recent history. A devaluation of the pound sterling was actively expected in 1964, but failed to occur; in 1967, devaluation resulted from a brief period of currency disturbance lasting scarcely more than two months, after a year in which a parity change was generally discounted. The devaluation of the French franc in August 1969 came at an almost wholly unexpected date, as was also the case for the previous devaluation in 1957. A period of considerable speculation as to whether the Deutsche Mark would be revalued, or whether exchange controls would be introduced by the West German Republic, ended in April 1971 with the introduction of neither of these measures, but with a floating of the rate. Whereas an earlier change in the par value of the German Mark, in 1969, had not been followed, for instance, by the Swiss franc, the latter currency moved with the Mark, against expectations, in 1971. The Smithsonian settlement of December 18th 1971 brought with it widespread currency changes affecting many countries, and involving a variety of new parities, not all of which could be foreseen with accuracy. The floating, rather than the devaluation, of the pound in June 1972 was generally surprising, not only in the nature of the choice, but also in the date at which this was made. The simultaneous floating of the rand, in contrast to the events of 1967, was also broadly unexpected.

(*b*) ACTION IN RELATION TO PAR VALUE CHANGES

It remains now to consider in more detail the precise courses of action open to the parent company where a change in the par value of its subsidiaries' currency appears imminent. For this purpose the contingency of devaluation will be taken, bearing in mind that effects opposite those described will occur in the event of revaluation. Given the analysis in the foregoing, it would appear simplest to consider possible parent action under the headings of the three main fund flows in question, i.e. (a) capital transfers from the parent; (b) income remittances from the subsidiary; (c) extension of trade credit by the subsidiary to the parent. The implications for asset positions and for other fund flows can be considered as they become relevant to the above three headings.

These actions will be investigated in two forms. Firstly, the managerial considerations for and against each method of protection will be considered. Secondly, an attempt will be made with the aid of available data to quantify the exact effect of these procedures, both on the companies and on the balance of payments of the countries concerned.

(i) Capital Transfers from the Parent

Replacement of Parent's Capital

The prime characteristic of parent's capital is perhaps that it is a relatively small but essential part of the financing of the subsidiary. The charts on pages 54–55 and 58–59 of Part I show that in both developed and developing countries, parent funds form a minor proportion of subsidiaries' total sources of funds. However, parents' funds will, in developing countries, constitute an accretion of capital which in most cases can neither be supplied from the cash flow of the subsidiary itself, nor from the capital market of the country in which the subsidiary is situated. In the case of developed countries, where the local capital market is per se more abundant, the same basic observation will apply; parent's capital will only come into play when the internal resources of the subsidiary and those of its local capital market have been fully exploited. If, therefore, the contribution of parent capital is to be curtailed in the interests of avoiding devaluation losses, the financial managers of the company will be confronted with the task of finding substitute funds. By definition, from the above analysis, fresh funds are unlikely to be forthcoming from the local capital market. Similarly, the requisite financing is not to be sought in further internal resources of the subsidiary. A supplementary margin of internal resources could be made available through higher retentions; that is to say, through a reduction in the level of dividends remitted to the parent; the extra funds so withheld could be devoted to the capital needs in question. However, this procedure would manifestly fall foul of another desideratum *vis-à-vis* devaluation risks: the increase in remittances of dividends to the parent. Another source of replacement funds might be the local banking sector. However, it is clear that the funds required are long-term in nature, normally, for the financing of a new investment project, and the acquisition of bank credit which can be retained for that period, or turned over sufficiently frequently, may be difficult, particularly in countries where banking practices remain traditional.

All in all, given that the need for parent company funds will arise when a capital project is to be undertaken, and other sources of finance have already been fully employed, the decision to dispense with the parent's equity or loan contribution is bound to be a difficult one. Whilst in many cases the problems involved may be overcome, it is equally likely that if the decision is to be adhered to, then the capital project itself will have to be shelved or postponed.

Given the difficulty of altering investment plans, and the uncertainty as to the timing and magnitude of the causative event itself, it follows that in many companies, questions of par value changes are effectively given a lower priority than that of the capital project itself. The latter is frequently pursued in the calculated knowledge that a parity change may occur. In many cases the devaluation or revaluation materialises; in many other cases, however, it does not.

Accelerated Return of Loan Capital

It is appropriate, under this heading, to consider the question of the accelerated return by the subsidiary of loan capital received in a past period from the parent. Many of the above factors will again come into play. It would be necessary for the subsidiary to have adequate means of financing this loss of capital, other than a reduction of profit remittances to the parent. It is worth bearing in mind at this point that a reduction of outstanding debt to the parent will also cause a fall in the latter's receipts of interest, an outcome not particularly desirable in face of a probable devaluation. However, where its subsidiary's financial position is good, and no capital projects are immediately outstanding, it may well be possible to arrange an accelerated payoff of loan capital.

(ii) Income Remittances from the Subsidiary

It follows from the foregoing that if dividend payments to the parent are to be accelerated, i.e. by instituting interim payments, then the funds for these payments must in principle come from the liquid short-term assets of the subsidiary.

Liquid Position of the Subsidiary

Both the financial principles common to all companies, and those appertaining especially to multi-company groups, as set out at the beginning of Part II above, militate against the accumulation of large liquid assets in subsidiary companies. The finances of any company are used for the transmission of resources through the whole business process—from the acquisition of raw materials through the manufacturing process, to the distribution and sale of the product. It is inherent in any efficient discharge of this function that surplus amounts of readily available financial assets should not arise; these should be put to investment or operating use as expeditiously as possible. The essence of the multi-company function is furthermore that surplus funds should not be left in member companies of the group, but should be transmitted to the parent for reallocation in capital form to other needy areas of the group, or for distribution in the form of profits to the ultimate shareholders of the group. On both these counts, therefore, it is not to be expected that a high level of liquid assets will be present in a subsidiary company at any particular time.

Local Borrowing

If augmented profit remittances to the parent are therefore to be undertaken, this will normally be done through an increase in the subsidiary's trade and bank credit in its own country. This is in itself a desirable recourse, since it both channels assets to the parent, and increases the parent's contingent liabilities in the country subject to a devaluation risk. Wherever possible, this redeployment of short-term funds is carried out by international companies.

The degree to which this is possible is determined largely by the amount of credit available, and the terms under which it may be procured. In developing countries, there will be a finite limit to the amount of bank credit which can be obtained. In developed countries, banking funds are relatively abundant. However, it frequently occurs that in a country exposed to parity pressures, credit control measures may have been taken by the government which have the effect either of physically restricting the advances available, or of significantly raising their cost. The finance manager of the international company then has a delicate problem of alternative cost to resolve. He must decide whether the extra interest cost of borrowing locally will be equal to or will exceed the loss in the exchange value of the same sum of money if this is remitted in the form of profit after devaluation. To cite a simple numerical example: let it be supposed that a subsidiary borrows $100 from its local bank in the January of one year, to remit this in the form of early dividends to its parent. The bank's interest charge is 10 per cent annually. If the anticipated devaluation takes place almost immediately after the transfer of the dividends, and if it is by a margin of 10 per cent, then the international group will have gained nothing from the subsidiary's actions; and if the bank loan is not repaid at the end of the year, would indeed have lost. If the anticipated devaluation does not, in fact, materialise immediately, and does not take place in fact until the end of the year, then the international group would have been better advised to allow its subsidiary to do nothing at all, but simply pay its dividends at the due date; then devaluation loss will be equal to the bank interest which would have been paid. If devaluation had occurred at about the time expected, but was at a margin of 7 per cent or 5 per cent, then the subsidiary's action would have lost money for the group—assuming, as must be done, that the bank loan could not be repaid within the year; it follows that the bank loan was only incurred because other liquid resources, out of which the dividends might have been paid, were absent—therefore the bank loan is unlikely to be repaid. If, again, devaluation ensues at a punctual date, and at a margin above 10 per cent—say 15 per cent—then the subsidiary's action will have saved money for the group. However, if devaluation at 15 per cent does not take place until the end of the year, then the saving will only be 5 per cent; and if the bank loan is not repaid within eighteen months, then the saving will be erased. Of course, in any eventuality the parent will gain from the accelerated receipt of a dividend. However, this gain is short-lived, since the early payment—made only for the purpose of minimising a devaluation loss—will be succeeded by an extra-long period without dividend.

The decision as to whether to pay accelerated dividends on the proceeds of local borrowing rests, therefore, on an exact judgement of the timing and extent of the expected devaluation, both seen in relation to the likely interest charged by the bank. Essentially, the financial manager must organise the transaction in such a way as to ensure both that the bank interest payable is less than the devaluation margin, and that devaluation is not delayed beyond the time scale implicit in the differential between the devaluation and interest rate (viz. eighteen months for a five point differential with a 10 per cent bank interest rate; two years for a ten point differential with a 10 per cent bank interest rate).

Clearly, a diversion of borrowed liquid assets into higher dividend payments can effectively mitigate the loss on devaluation. However, the success of the operation rests on the judgement on the part of the group's financial managers of the timing and scope of the devaluation—matters not lending themselves, as explained above, to easy prediction.

Income Transfers other than by Dividends

It is appropriate to mention at this point that the other methods of transferring earnings from the subsidiary to the parent, which were treated above under the heading of taxation, and include payments of managerial fees, royalties, loan interest and transfer price procedures, may also be brought into play in relation to exchange risk pre-emption. The relatively small potential for royalty and fee payments has already been described. Loan interest payments are, by their nature, inflexible, and dependent on the loan policy of the parent in a past period. They can therefore hardly be raised or lowered in response to a relatively short-term necessity such as that represented by forthcoming parity changes. Moreover, the concurrent pressure on the parent to reduce its loan capital in the subsidiary would tend to check, rather than enlarge, loan interest payments. The practical considerations surrounding the use of transfer price mechanisms have already been dealt with, and need not be reiterated. It suffices to mention, in the present context, that the shifting of profits through an adjustment of transfer prices is necessarily a continuing process, and is not easily adapted to the relatively speedy repatriation of profits from the subsidiary which a devaluation contingency would require.

(iii) Extension of Trade Credit by the Subsidiary to the Parent

The main purpose of this is to avert losses in the proceeds of current sales from the parent to the subsidiary. It is also, as explained above, a method of allowing the parent company to generate a short-term liability in the country of impending devaluation—long-term liabilities being effectively excluded. The efficacy of the device will depend, as has already been remarked, upon the level of trade between the parent and the subsidiary. Where this is not significant, an insubstantial liability only will be accumulated. However, where trade is reasonably large, it is open to the subsidiary to defer invoices on its exports to the parent, thus permitting a liability in favour of the parent to grow on its books. Similarly, the subsidiary will meet promptly invoices on deliveries of goods from the parent, thus excluding the build-up of a parent's asset on their books.

Leads and Lags

The above-mentioned procedure is merely an example of the familiar phenomenon of leads and lags, and might best be considered in that context. The basic principle of leads and lags is that debit balances should be built up in the weak currency through the delayed payment of exports from that country, and the accelerated payment for imports into that country. It is not, of course, necessary that leading and lagging should be confined to parent/subsidiary trade. At least theoretical formulae can be worked out, whereby suitable use of this procedure between various subsidiaries of the same group can lead to sizeable savings in the event of parity changes. Thus if subsidiary (B) is receiving raw materials from subsidiary (A), and delivering finished products to subsidiary (C), and a 10 per cent devaluation occurs in the currency of subsidiary (B), and if the level of trade between the subsidiaries was $100 per month in each case, then if three months' leading and lagging is practised by all the parties: at the date of devaluation subsidiary (B) will avoid the loss of $30 (on $300 worth of imports) and subsidiary (C) will ensure its gain of $30 on its imports from subsidiary (B). The foregoing illustration, of course, assumes that all transactions are conducted in the currency of the exporter. Where this is not so, appropriate leads and lags can none the less be practised.

A number of points are worth noting in relation to the practice of leading and lagging. Firstly, the nicety of timing required for the dividend and other fund movements mentioned above is not required. Leading and lagging can be carried on continuously on a two-month, three-month, or other time basis until the parity change actually occurs, when the leads and lags can then be unwound with the exchange benefits described. However, the duration of leads and lags is controlled in most countries, and a legal limit is applied beyond which it is impossible to go. A further important limitation is that both in the case of delays in payment by the parent of the subsidiary's bills, and in acceleration of payment by the subsidiary of the parent's bills, sufficient liquidity will need to be on hand to finance the operation. The subsidiary will require sufficient liquid funds to allow it to await receipt of the parent's payment, or to permit it to meet the parent's bills early. Where, as is probable, this liquidity is not available, resort will have to be had to short-term borrowing. In this instance the financial managers of the company will, again, have to weigh up the alternative costs of bank credit and devaluation losses along the lines described for the financing of accelerated remittances of dividends.

Secondly, leading and lagging gives protection for the transaction immediately affected by the parity change; all subsequent transactions bear the full devaluation or revaluation impact.

Thirdly, the benefit in the case of inter-subsidiary transactions will only become material to the group when the gains are transferred in the form of higher dividends to the parent company, as explained in other contexts above.

Fourthly, the efficacy of the method is dependent, in international company groups, on the degree of inter-trade between the group members.

Finally, it is perhaps worth noting that leading and lagging is a precaution applicable to all trade, and is by no means an exclusive prerogative of international companies. It will be apparent that leading and lagging, no matter what the denomination of the currency, or which side of the selling transaction is considered, will always be acceptable to both parties concerned. For instance, given an impending sterling devaluation, UK importers from independent suppliers in the United States would meet the dollar invoices on such consignments without delay, so as to avoid paying the extra amount of sterling needed to cover the dollar amount following upon devaluation. Similarly, where UK exporters invoiced in sterling to independent company recipients in the United States, the American company would seek the longest permissible payment delay, so as to increase its chances of a reduced bill in dollar terms consequent upon devaluation. In the case of the UK import transaction, the United States supplier will naturally not resist early settlement for his shipment of goods. Similarly, in the case of UK exports, the United States recipient will not normally be pressed for early payment, since the devaluation contingency is immaterial to the UK exporter. Should the UK exporter not wish, perhaps for liquidity reasons, to wait for payment, it is open to him to borrow sterling locally in the ordinary way. The cost of the latter will be balanced by the premium he will charge on his export invoice. Trade credit between unrelated companies is not, like that of international group companies, normally free of interest.

Assuming that the currency of settlement is not that of the exporter, similar leads and lags effects take place. In the first transaction mentioned above, where the British imports from the US are invoiced in sterling, the British importer will not hasten his payment, but the American exporter will sell the sterling proceeds forward at the date of invoice. In the same way should, in the second case, the British consignment be invoiced in dollars, then the American importer—for whom the devaluation contingency is immaterial—will pay at the fullest possible maturity date, in which he will not be resisted by the UK exporter.

Thus it is apparent that at times of expected parity change, leads and lags occur over the whole trade of the country of the currency concerned, regardless of the currency in which the invoices are settled, and regardless of the relationship between the companies engaged in the trade.

Covering

It is perhaps appropriate in this context to refer to the use of forward currency purchases to diminish the risk of loss upon currency changes. This is a matter perhaps a further stage removed from the subject of parents' short-term liabilities in subsidiaries' countries, opened at the beginning of this section. This operation will not normally enter into the settlement of trade invoices between members of international groups, where leading and lagging based on intra-company liabilities will be used. Forward covering will come into play in the trade of a subsidiary with other non-affiliated companies.

Forward covering, in fact, affects the subsidiary's ability to maintain a profitable trade in general, in face of parity changes, and refers more to the overall profitability of the subsidiary, as described on page 113 above. However, the point perhaps arises naturally in the discussion regarding the reaction of traders to currency changes, and may usefully be mentioned here.

Forward covering consists in the buying in advance of currency needed to meet a given transaction. Covering will typically be done by importers in a devaluation-prone country of goods invoiced in a foreign currency, or by exporters of goods to a devaluation-prone country of goods invoiced in the latter country's currency; the remaining alternative situations are evident. Thus, to assume a possible sterling devaluation, British importers obtaining goods from, say, Switzerland will on the conclusion of the contract buy at once the Swiss francs needed for the payment of the consignment, rather than wait until delivery of the invoice in, say, three months' time, during which interval the pound may have suffered a devaluation. Swiss francs obtained in this manner are available only at a premium, since the supplier of the francs must himself take on the devaluation risk. Two points are to be noted in respect to this procedure.

Firstly, the question of timing is again important. To take a simple example: let it be supposed that a British importer engaged in regular trade with Switzerland obtains ten deliveries each year, invoiced at £10 each. The three-month forward premium for Swiss francs is 7 per cent per annum. Let it also be supposed that the pound is eventually devalued by a margin of 7 per cent. It is clear that the British importers' loss on any uncovered consignment overtaken by devaluation will be:

$$\frac{£10 \times 7}{100} = 70p.$$

Therefore, any forward covering involving the importer in forward premia totalling 70p. or more will leave him in a neutral or in a loss position. In the present case, of course, any forward covering operation involving one consignment or more will bring about this result. Thus the operation of forward covering, to be effective, must be dependent on the correct judgement of the importer as to the timing and the extent of the devaluation to be forestalled. Overlong covering, or covering at rates unduly high in relation to the devaluation rate actually incurred, will bring about a loss.

The same principle applies, of course, but in the reverse direction, to exporters whose currency is expected to be revalued. The principle is modified but still applies where the forward exchange market receives official support; this will be described in further detail under (*d*) SPECULA-TION (p. 136).

The second point is that forward covering can only provide once-for-all protection. It can secure the importer or exporter against the loss on the transaction immediately following the change of parity. However, the regular trader cannot be relieved of the loss attendant on all subsequent transactions.

(*c*) STATISTICAL EFFECTS OF ACTION IN RELATION TO PAR VALUE CHANGES

As has been seen, international companies, faced with possible changes in the currencies of the countries in which they operate, may reduce flows of capital to subsidiaries and increase repayments of capital from subsidiaries; increase payments by subsidiaries of dividends and other income; increase subsidiaries' borrowing in the local capital market, particularly at short-term; increase the subsidiaries' trade credit to the parent.

These are the major operations which it will be desirable for the inter-national group to undertake, in face of devaluation or revaluation risks. However, as suggested in the foregoing, the feasibility in practice of the operations will depend on the other circumstances of the group, and in particular on the state of capital investment projects at the time, and of the overall financial structure of the subsidiary. It remains to be seen how these two elements of management decision are resolved in practice.

Where these protective operations can be mounted, then the second question arising is that of the effect of these practices upon the national financial environment in which they occur. Changes in capital and income flows between subsidiaries and parents will impinge upon the general balance of payments of the countries concerned, and may have a greater or lesser effect on these. The same will be true of the changes in trade credit and in leads and lags. Increased borrowing by the subsidiaries may or may not affect the general level of credit in the country in which the subsidiary operates.

These questions can be resolved only on the evidence of the figures.

The type of data necessary to explore this area of enquiry must consist not only of figures for the transfer of capital between a representative sample of parent companies and subsidiaries, but also of payments of dividends, interest, royalties and fees by the subsidiaries; of changes in leads and lags between international group members; and of long- and short-term borrowing by the subsidiaries in the local market. In addition, the data should apply to a sequence of years in which a devaluation or revaluation contingency was present, and in which fluctuation in these financial aggregates in response to this contingency might be identified. This involves a highly specific choice of data.

For these reasons a body of statistics has been assembled, and is presented below, on the experience of companies in the UK during the years 1960–70, and in the German Federal Republic between 1969 and 1971. These particular series have been used for two reasons. Firstly, the type of information required is sparse, and is in fact available for only a few industrialised countries. Secondly, the UK and West Germany appear to be particularly well-suited examples of the processes under observation. Both countries contain a high degree of international company activity distributed over a wide range of industrial sectors. Both countries have highly-developed long-term capital markets from which international companies are not rigorously excluded. They also have well-developed banking systems providing the short-term borrowing and currency exchange facilities required. Their exchange control is not such as substantially to impede the financial operations in question.

Above all, the two countries are good examples—perhaps the most prominent in recent years—of situations where par value changes are expected; in the one case the parity change anticipated was in the sense of a devaluation; in the other, in the sense of revaluation.

It appears therefore suitable to use the experience of these two countries as a model of what might happen elsewhere; indeed it might be assumed that the financial response to parity changes in these countries fully reflects, where it does not exceed, any response possible elsewhere. The degree of anticipation of change was more intense in these countries than elsewhere; the number of companies likely to respond as great or greater; the financial machinery and facilities as extensive or more extensive.

(i) Professor Lee Remmers' Data

The following table shows the movements of four of the main financial aggregates (bank credit, long-term borrowing, funds from the parent, dividends paid to the parent) in a major sample of British companies.[2] The sample comprises one hundred and fifteen subsidiaries, located in

[2] That used by Professor Lee Remmers in his study *The Strategy of Multinational Enterprise* (see Part I, page 60).

the UK, of large international companies: 90 of which had their head-quarters in the United States, and 25 of which had parent companies in other countries of Western Europe.[3]

Year	Bank Credit raised in UK (1)	Long-term Debts raised in UK (2)	Equity and Loan Funds from the Parent or the Group (3)	Dividends paid to the Parent (4)	£000 change in year Net Cash Flow (retained earnings after tax + depreciation provisions) (5)
1960	16,868	5,805	12,604	30,807	50,058
1961	8,938	2,177	28,672	41,801	41,064
1962	6,786	3,889	32,252	33,145	52,753
1963	−2,964	5,597	24,521	36,931	71,138
1964	43,108	11,078	22,960	48,592	80,003
1965	50,441	21,339	23,784	40,046	109,490
1966	9,563	27,519	17,780	43,658	105,125
1967	975	9,028	44,515	44,169	135,976
1968	28,251	16,704	31,434	43,542	153,278

The table records the extent to which this large sample of subsidiary companies actually practised the protective operations discussed above—i.e. the generation of local liabilities, the reduction of fresh capital receipts from the parent, and the repatriation of liquid assets to the parent in the form of dividends—over most of the 1960s and particularly in the two years 1964 and 1967: one of high devaluation expectation, and the other of actual devaluation. The table deserves consideration in detail.

As regards bank credit: it will be seen that there were widespread changes over the years from an increase of some £50 m. in 1965 to a decrease of some £3 m. in 1963. Bank borrowing of £43 m. in 1964 was certainly greater than that in the previous two or three years, although it was not as great as in the immediately following year. On the other hand, bank borrowing in 1967, the year of actual devaluation, was unusually small, and in 1968, the year following devaluation, the increase was not of a particularly high order.

Moving on to long-term debt, similar impressions emerge. The increase in debt in 1964 was greater than in the previous three years, but it was not as great as in the following two years, and in 1967, the year of actual devaluation, the increase in debt was very small.

[3] The table is compiled from the disaggregated figures by company and by year for each item, kindly supplied by Professor Lee Remmers from his own data for the purpose of the present study.

Receipts of new capital from the parent fell moderately in 1964 as against 1963, but rose sharply in 1967 as against 1966.

Dividend payments to the parent did not increase particularly sharply in the two critical years; 1964 remittances were higher than 1963, but not markedly higher than, for instance, 1961. In 1967 they were of about the same volume as 1966 and 1968, and were slightly below that of 1964.

The table as a whole does not appear, in fact, to suggest a pattern of reactions to exchange risks. Indeed, examination of the individual results of each company in each year show that the annual totals are merely an arithmetic aggregation of individual operations varying very widely, and without apparent common causation, both as regards their actual size and as regards the direction of their movement.

Where any pattern is discernible, it is perhaps in the broad movement of the capital and income items over the years. Thus net cash flow moved steadily up between 1960 and 1968, increasing by some 300 per cent. Dividends increased by about 140 per cent and capital inflows from the parent grew less smoothly, but overall by some 250–300 per cent. These trends may be thought to reflect the gradual expansion of the enterprises in the course of ordinary business over the period. On the other hand, the size of liabilities, particularly those at short-term, was, as the nature of the item might imply, both inconstant and unreflective of any apparent trend.

(ii) British Official Data

Capital and Income Flows

The evidence gathered by Professor Lee Remmers appears to be borne out by data available from official sources. The following table shows data collected by the UK Department of Trade and Industry over the years 1963–70 for United Kingdom subsidiaries and affiliates of foreign enterprises in all industrial and commercial sectors except oil.

Year	Interest Paid (1)	Dividends Paid (2)	Receipts of Share & Loan Capital (3)
1963	3	66	49
1964	5	108	69
1965	6	97	51
1966	6	90	73
1967	7	93	56
1968	9	114	123
1969	9	131	114
1970	10	118	90

SOURCE: *Business Monitor M4*, Overseas Transactions, Department of Trade and Industry, April 1971.

Interest payments by subsidiaries in the UK show a steady progression over the period, with no marked jump either in 1964 or in 1967. There was some increase in dividends paid in 1964, but this again was not large in comparison with the apparent trend over the years 1964–70; again, in 1967 there was no particular increase. As regards new share and loan capital from the parent, 1964 showed a slight increase rather than a decrease; 1967 a decrease, but one mainly in relation to the slightly augmented figure for 1966. Examination of the dividend totals suggests the possibility that companies were taken by surprise when sterling was devalued in 1967, and may have been repatriating dividends at a higher level in the subsequent years 1968 and 1969, out of the fear that devaluation might be repeated. This supposition, however, conflicts with the evidence on new capital flows from the parents shown in the third column, since these increased rather than decreased in 1968 and 1969.

Trade Credit

Further official data published in the United Kingdom throws ligh the extent of trade credit adjustments between members of international companies based in the UK and their affiliates abroad. The following table summarises the position for the years 1964 to 1969:

						Change in amounts due[4]
	Trade Credit of UK-based Parents and Subsidiaries of International Companies					
			£m.			
	1964	*1965*	*1966*	*1967*	*1968*	*1969*
Credit Given	−28	−42	−11	−11	−20	−64
Credit Received	+54	+23	+10	−10	+16	+74
	Trade Credit of Unrelated UK Companies and Banks					
Credit Given	−48	−62	−169	−187	−331	−328
Credit Received	+3	+13	−4	+26	+82	+97
	Total Trade Credit					
Credit Given	−76	−104	−180	−198	−351	−392
Credit Received	+57	+36	+6	+16	+98	+171

SOURCE: *United Kingdom Balance of Payments*, HMSO Central Statistical Office, 1971, Table 47.

The first section in the above table constitutes a numerical statement of the leads and lags operations discussed earlier, above. 'Credit given' is credit extended by UK-based subsidiaries of international companies,

[4] *Assets:* increase −/decrease +. *Liabilities:* increase +/decrease −.

or UK-based parents of international companies on exports to their affiliates in the group outside the United Kingdom. 'Credit Received' is credit received by UK companies on imports from affiliates outside the United Kingdom. The table is expressed in balance of payments terms, i.e. extensions of credits on exports are shown with a minus sign, and extensions of credits on imports are shown as a plus. Reductions of credit on both sides are shown by the reversals of the sign.

As was stated above, if leads and lags are practised at a time of impending devaluation of the pound, large increases in credit given (minus sign) and marked decreases in credit received (also minus sign) might be expected. As will be seen, this was not the case in 1964. Lags by UK-based companies —i.e. extension of credit on their exports to affiliates abroad—increased in 1964 less than in 1965. In 1967 the increase was one of the smallest in the period. Similarly, a reduction in credit received on imports might have been expected; however, in 1964 there was a sizeable increase in credit accepted by British-based companies on imports from foreign affiliates, although in 1967 there was a small reduction.

Further interest lies in the two following sections of the table; i.e. the sections entitled 'Trade Credit of Unrelated UK Companies and Banks', and 'Total Trade Credit'. These two sections, as the names imply, show leads and lags firstly between UK businesses not members of international companies, and trading with independent firms abroad; and secondly, leads and lags operated by all companies, i.e. independent companies and members of international groups combined.

It will be seen in the case of unrelated companies that, again, no special link with devaluation risks can be identified. Export credit grew steadily over the period. Import credit was certainly small in 1964, but was not actually reduced until 1966. Import credit was again growing, although moderately, in 1967.

The above table therefore fails to demonstrate any distinct leads and lags practices related to exchange risks. Indeed, the table appears to reflect more clearly the gradual growth of export credit—a characteristic of industrial exporting countries over the period. However, it should be borne in mind that the table is not necessarily conclusive. Leads and lags in relation to currency changes are believed normally to be of short duration. It is therefore quite possible that fairly sizeable fluctuations, bringing some pressure on the balance of payments, occurred within the yearly periods shown.

The second point of interest attaching to the above table lies in the comparative size of leads and lags by international companies, and by independents. As will be seen, movements of import credit in international companies were fairly large in relation to the total at the beginning of the period, but were small at the end. Movements of export credit were a small part of the total throughout. This point is borne out more clearly in other data provided by the United Kingdom Government statistical service on the total amount of credit actually in existence at any given time, and summarised in the following table:

Total Trade Credit Outstanding End-1969

	Export Credit Given £m.	Import Credit Received £m.
International	488	360
Independent[5]	1,936	384
Total	2,424	744

Source: *United Kingdom Balance of Payments*, Central Statistical Office hmso, 1971, Table 46.

It is important, as the footnote to the above table indicates, to separate trade credit practised by international groups through the medium of intra-company liabilities, from that practised by the same groups through the medium of facilities obtained from banks. The purpose of the present study is to isolate those areas where, by reason of their interconnected character, member companies of international groups create financial flows not arising between unrelated companies. For this reason, trade credit operated by means of intra-company liabilities is the sole flow attributable to international groups as such. Where member companies of these groups resort to trade credit obtainable from banks, then they are acting irrespective of the mechanisms available to them through their group's financial arrangements, and are obtaining facilities alongside all other companies in the open market; indeed it is probable that trade credit obtained by international group members from banks is in favour of trade with unrelated companies outside the group.

As the table shows, the total amount of export credit outstanding at the end of 1969 was £2,424 m. Of this, £1,936 m. was between independent companies. Thus export lags were practised by the different companies in the following proportions: 80 per cent by independent companies; 20 per cent by international companies. For import leads, the figures were: total credit received £744 m., of which £384 m. was between independent companies. Percentage relationship: independent companies 52 per cent; international companies 48 per cent.

Thus international companies appeared to hold a relatively small share of export claims, and a larger—although still not the major—share of import liabilities. At the same time, as the immediately preceding table showed, the movements in these claims and liabilities appeared to be less volatile than in those of independent companies.

[5] Including banks and including trade credit by banks to members of international company groups.

(iii) Bundesbank Data

The quantification of fund movements *vis-à-vis* exchange rate changes cannot be concluded without a reference to the excellent series of statistics recently produced by the German Bundesbank.[6] The enquiry giving rise to these statistics was focussed on the period 1969 to 1971, a sequence of years in which the German Mark was 'revaluation prone'; i.e. the parity was generally expected to be raised in relation to other currencies.

It follows from what has been said earlier above that in these circumstances, international companies—and indeed other parties outside Germany—are likely to try to increase their assets in German Marks; and at the same time German-based companies are likely to increase their liabilities in foreign currencies.

The Bundesbank Report examines the state of external short- and long-term liabilities of German-based companies in the period end-1969 to August 1971. These liabilities comprised purely long- and short-term borrowings; owing to statistical difficulties it was not possible to include trade credit. The following table summarises the statistics compiled by the Bundesbank:

			Liabilities outstanding[7]
			DMm.[8]
	End 1969	*End May 1971*	*End August 1971*
Short-term Liabilities			
Independent[9]	1,800		7,800
International[10]	1,700[11] (3,800)	N/A	5,200 (11,400)
Total	5,600	20,900	19,200
Long-term Liabilities			
Independent	N/A	N/A	9,600
International	N/A	N/A	4,800
Total	5,200	12,400	14,400
Grand Total	10,800	33,300	33,600

In considering the above, it should be borne in mind that the period of expectation of revaluation ended on 10th May, 1971, when the German Mark was floated. As will be seen, the total external liabilities of German-based companies increased rapidly over the period, from DM 10·8 bn. to

[6] *German enterprises foreign debt*, Monthly Report of the Deutsche Bundesbank, November 1971, page 19.
[7] Gross; i.e. not net of claims.
[8] Rounded to nearest DM 100 m.
[9] German-based companies not affiliated to companies abroad.
[10] German-based companies affiliated either as subsidiaries or parents to companies abroad. Figures shown are only for inter-company liabilities; total liabilities (including those to banks) are shown in brackets.
[11] Estimated.

DM 33·6 bn. The greatest increase was in short-term liabilities: these grew from DM 5·6 bn. to DM 19·2 bn.

The table, however, demonstrates two points rather clearly. The first of these is that international companies took a relatively small share of the total accumulation of liabilities: 30 per cent at the end of 1969, and 27 per cent in August 1971.

The second point is that the inclusion of figures for May 1971, i.e. the date of revaluation, and for August 1971, permits the calculation of the purely speculative element in the fund movements to Germany. Those funds which were placed in Germany solely for the purpose of a capital gain on revaluation would have been moved out after the Mark was floated in May 1971. As will be seen, by the end of August 1971, total short-term liabilities had fallen to DM 19·2 bn. Thus it appears that of the total increase in liabilities from the end of 1969 to May 1971—DM 15·2 bn. —DM 1·7 bn., or 11 per cent, were speculative in character. Unfortunately a figure for international companies' liabilities at the end of May 1971 is not available, but it may safely be assumed that the speculative element would have been similar.

That the speculative element was small was borne out by the Bundesbank's comments in the article. It remarked: 'The main reason for the increase in enterprises' foreign indebtedness was probably the rise in the credit requirement of German trade and industry' and went on to show how the stringent domestic monetary policies applied by the German authorities had led to a large growth in the financial deficit of German enterprises, and at the same time to a rise in German interest rates to levels considerably above those of other countries and of the international capital market. Given the freedom allowed to movements of capital into Germany, companies met their financial requirements with greater ease and at lower cost by the resort to foreign borrowed funds. That this was so is also borne out by the fact that some 38 per cent of total foreign liabilities was denominated in foreign currencies, and by the fact that the rate of long-term borrowing continued high in the period following the events of May 1971.

The Bundesbank, it should be noted, refers in its article to the period from the beginning of 1969 until the revaluation of the German Mark in October 1969, during which German enterprises' short-term external liabilities grew by some DM 6 bn., a total of funds which was almost fully expatriated after the revaluation. However, no data is furnished in respect of international companies.

(iv) Conclusions on Statistics

In the discussions pursued in the foregoing sections prior to that on statistics, the losses confronting international companies upon the devaluation of any of the currencies in which they were operating were portrayed; at the same time, the dispositions which these companies might take to lessen these losses were described, together with the difficulties by which these dispositions might be attended. Lastly, it was remarked that most if not all arrangements were precautionary rather than enduring in character, since the ultimate loss attendant upon a change in parities was ineluctable.

It remained for the evidence of the figures to show which of the two main alternatives available to companies prevailed; that is to say, whether international companies at all costs avoided currency losses, or whether, in recognition of the difficulties involved and the ultimate logic of parity changes, their response was selective and partial only.

The figures which it has been possible to assemble in the section immediately above seem to indicate (although incomplete) that the second of these alternatives was followed, in general, by the companies. Although in many cases international companies no doubt adjusted capital flows, dividend payments, and short- and long-term liabilities, with decisive if not spectacular effect for their profitability in the face of currency changes, it appears that their aggregate actions were not such as to produce a discernible effect on financial flows, still less an effect upon the balance of payments of the countries in which they were operating.

(*d*) SPECULATION

Speculation is a currency operation. However, it is important to notice that not all currency operations are speculations. A number of currency operations open to international companies have already been mentioned above; these include hedging, covering, and leading and lagging. These transactions have a specific *raison d'être* relating to the company's business operations and, to the extent to which they are practised, serve to reduce as far as possible losses in the value of capital assets, current assets, and sales returns caused by changes in par values.

By 'speculation' should be understood a currency operation undertaken per se for the sake of its inherent gain, unconnected with the business operations of the firm in question. The definition used by a leading expert is perhaps helpful in this context: 'The creation and maintenance of short positions in foreign exchanges solely for the purpose of being able to earn a capital profit, if the currencies concerned should be devalued or if they should appreciate.'[11]

Typical examples of the kind of operation envisaged are the selling short of devaluation-prone currencies, and the acquisition of short-term holdings of currencies likely to appreciate. Thus a company might

[11] Paul Einzig: *Foreign Exchange Crises*, Macmillan, London; St. Martin's Press, New York, 1968.

undertake to provide sterling at a short-term future date, i.e. in three months' time, at a price at which, if devaluation intervened, would furnish it with a capital gain. For example: if sterling were sold at three months at $2·70 to the £1 in October 1967, then the sterling funds could have been provided at the due date in January 1968 at $2·40 to the £1, thus enabling the company to make a capital gain of 30¢ on each £1 supplied. Alternatively, spot sterling—either the property of the operator or the proceeds of a short-term sterling loan—could have been sold for $2·80 to the £1 in October 1967; the sterling could then have been repurchased at $2·40 and the loan repaid after devaluation. A number of variants of the above procedures exist. All, however, rest on the basic principle of securing short-term assets in currencies likely to appreciate, and short-term liabilities in currencies likely to depreciate.

It should first be noted that the practice of speculation is a good deal less simple than is suggested by the bare outline shown above. In the first place, official support of the forward exchange in national currencies lessens the margin of speculative gain; thus in the case of sterling, as mentioned on page 127 above, Bank of England forward operations reduced the margin between spot and forward rates to some 1 per cent a year prior to 1967. Secondly, exchange controls in many countries prohibit residents from speculating in their own currencies.

A further point worth noting is that speculation rests upon the availability either of liquid assets or of borrowed funds. It has been seen that in the case of subsidiary companies, liquid assets are, in devaluation-prone countries, remitted to the parent company in the form of dividends and other earnings as expeditiously as possible. Borrowed funds, where available, are used to facilitate this purpose. It seems safe to assume that in all cases where liquid assets arise in a subsidiary company, the currency of which is likely to depreciate, the parent company will wish to see these returned in the form of income rather than allow them to be used for speculative purposes. In the first case avoidance of a devaluation loss is certain; in the second case benefit from a short-term transaction is putative.

Both on the score of exchange control and of the best use of funds, it seems likely, therefore, that speculation by subsidiaries is for practical purposes non-existent. It would remain for the parent companies to operate with their own funds, either in the Eurocurrency markets or directly in the national currencies concerned. However, since the parent companies of most international groups—being located either in North America or Western Europe—are themselves in many cases subject to the exchange control regulations of their own governments, the scope here is again reduced. Speculation appears open only to parent companies based in countries free of exchange control, or in suitably located international base companies. These companies will therefore, if they are to speculate, divert part of their liquid assets to the purchase, for example, of short-term Deutsche Mark holdings at times when that currency appears likely to appreciate, or will sell sterling in the short-term forward market, or borrow spot sterling at short-term, when that currency is exposed to devaluation.

It might be felt that possession of funds for this purpose is not necessary, since forward exchange transactions require no credit, and for transactions where credit is required the company concerned could operate, for instance, with borrowed Eurodollars. However, it should be borne in mind at this point that the principle of speculation is to secure an overall gain over a number of individual operations, any of which, in the nature of the activity, may produce a loss. Successful speculation depends on an exact assessment of the timing and nature of the par value change involved, and—as has been mentioned earlier—which judgement is inherently difficult. Parity changes are essentially political decisions, and depart both in timing and in content from what may be judged likely on economic or financial grounds. Thus it is likely that a good deal of speculative funds were used for the short-selling of the pound in 1964 without profits. Similarly, it could be supposed that speculators having bought German Marks with Swiss francs in 1969, and secured a capital gain on the revaluation of the German Mark in that year, might have acted similarly prior to the floating of the German Mark in May 1971; however, in this case the Swiss franc floated by an equivalent amount, and any speculative gain was eliminated.

The parent or international base company engaged in speculation will therefore, whether using no credit, or whether using its own or Euro-currency funds, need to operate on the basis of a 'float' obtained from its own liquid funds. It emerges from the above that a company indulging in speculation requires both the short-term or 'banking' funds and the professional expertise necessary for the activity.

The question therefore arises whether both speculative funds and speculative expertise are present to the extent required in international parent or base companies. This point may first be clarified by reference to a central characteristic of international companies mentioned at the beginning of the present Part. The financial service of a company cannot be said to hold funds in its own right. The financial flows of any company are no more than a translation into financial form of the resources of that company at any one time. Liquid assets, where these arise, are channelled as expeditiously as possible back into real resource uses of the company. There is no place in this schema for a permanent surplus of liquid assets, still less for a fund devoted to the operation of a currency speculation account.

It appears therefore that the practical scope for currency speculation by an international company is relatively small; nor is there any reason to suppose any willingness on the part of the management to make special arrangements to set aside funds for this purpose. Any funds so reserved would have to be withdrawn from the real resources of the company—thus lessening its ability to transact the business for which it was established.

Moreover, the funds so set aside would be devoted to a highly-skilled and professional activity. The finance department of the typical international company necessarily lacks personnel for the conduct of daily exchange arbitrage and forward transactions. In short, to attempt to enter this field would require the company to convert itself from an essentially manufacturing establishment, such as it was constituted, into an essentially banking establishment. This clearly is not a feasible proposition.

It follows therefore that purely speculative operations in currencies are not undertaken by international companies, and indeed are normally specifically prohibited in the internal financial regulations of the companies.

Where, in face of this, some individual managers may venture to essay a short-term gain for the company funds by use of speculative operations, the risks involved are manifest. Over any period of time, the possibilities of loss are as great as those of gain. A small speculative loss might not, in the medley of items incorporated in an international company's accounts, be noticeable; in this case, by the same token, the speculation is of little purpose. A large loss could, however, not be concealed; in this case the official concerned would be responsible to the Board and shareholders of the company for the misuse and loss of the company's funds.

CHAPTER 7

Recruitment of Capital

(a) DEFINITIONS

Questions of definitions are first of all important. When considering the recruitment of capital by international company groups, it should be borne in mind that the funds for consideration are either those raised by the subsidiaries themselves, or those transmitted by the parent to the subsidiaries. Capital raised by the parent company for its own internal use is by definition capital employed in the domestic business of the parent's country, and does not come within the purview of the present study. The analysis which follows will therefore be concerned with the capital financing of subsidiaries, either through the latter's local or international efforts, or through the passage of funds to them from the parent company.

As was evident from data already shown in the foregoing, investment capital recruited from sources external to the subsidiary (i.e. from the parent or from the local or international capital market) forms a small but vital part of the subsidiary's overall financing. It emerges from the data reproduced in Part I above[1] that this contribution amounts to some 20 per cent of the total sources of funds of subsidiaries, whether these be in developed or developing countries, or whether they be the dependents of parent companies in the US, the UK, or in other European countries. This is of course an average figure, and it should be noted that the capital funding of subsidiaries, particularly through the medium of parents' contributions, will be considerably above this average where the subsidiary is newly established.

The stability of the average ratio underlines the essential function of long-term capital input. Attention has been drawn earlier above to the basic principle of the financing of any business enterprise, whether this be unitary or multi-company in constitution, or domestic or international in deployment. Capital initiates resource-creating activity, furnishing earnings fairly soon in excess of the capital input: this autonomous generation of funds is sufficient to maintain the stock of assets created by

[1] Pages 53 *et seq.*

the initial investment, and indeed to contribute significantly towards new assets. Where frequent and substantial additions of assets are required, nevertheless, these internally generated funds are not normally sufficient. Thus where expanding enterprises are concerned, injections of new capital are invariably required. The foregoing is no more than a truism, expressing a well-known principle of financial management.

(*b*) THE EXTRA-TERRITORIAL POSTURE

However, when this principle is applied to the financial management of international corporations, a complication, already familiar under other headings in the present study, immediately arises. The international multi-company group is distinguished from other company groups solely through the fact that its component members are situated in different countries. The consequence of this for the recruitment of capital is that the subsidiaries of the multi-national company, although registered as national companies of the country in which they operate, none the less are, and are known to be, owned and controlled by a company foreign to that country. The capital recruited by these companies is therefore in principle capital supplied for a foreign user. In an equivalent and complementary way, capital recruited by the parent company in its own country for transmission to its subsidiaries abroad is, again, capital recruited for a foreign user. Thus in all its capital operations, wherever these may be conducted, the international company appears in the role of a foreign concern.

(*i*) *The Parent Company*

This notion requires some amplification. The parent company, raising capital in its domestic capital market, certainly appears as a domestic concern in the eyes of the investors who supply the capital. On the other hand, when it comes to transmit the proceeds of the capital-raising operation to its subsidiaries abroad, it does not so appear to its Government. It is now classed as an exporter of domestic capital, and will incur specific treatment on that score. In a number of countries, including the United States, the United Kingdom, France, and several other Western European countries, quantitative controls are applied to the amount of capital so exported. In the domestic capital market, furthermore, investors—whilst identifying the company as a domestic concern—will be guided in their readiness to furnish capital by their assessment of the prospects of the parent company's foreign affiliates, i.e. by the foreign end-uses of the capital being recruited.

(*ii*) *The Subsidiary*

In the case of the local recruitment of capital by subsidiaries, it remains true that a number of resident companies, although affiliates of foreign parents, are sufficiently strongly established and familiar members of the host country's business community to be assimilated entirely to the latter in the popular mind. Moreover in some countries, particularly in the developing areas, local affiliates of international companies may rank amongst the largest and most influential members of the local business community. This may be held to give them certain advantages in the raising of capital. Furthermore, where local affiliates are not in themselves particularly prominent, the reputation and financial strength of the parent company will be such that the latter's guarantee will serve to secure the affiliate's borrowing. Thus it might reasonably be held that subsidiaries of international companies, whether locally assimilated or not, and whether locally influential or not, are invariably in a favoured position with regard to the recruitment of local capital.

However, analysis of this proposition discloses a number of important qualifications. In the first place, foreign-owned subsidiaries that have merged into the local national scene will nevertheless retain their separate identity in the eyes of the government of that country, which will have precise knowledge of the proportion of equity held by the foreign parent. Whilst such a subsidiary might therefore receive support from the investors in the private capital market of that country, it will in many cases be subject to government-imposed ceilings on the level of borrowings to which it may resort. A number of governments, having in mind the balance of payments and the domestic capital resources of their countries, allow borrowing only pro rata to the input of new capital by the parent, or in accordance with other similar criteria. The capital markets of most countries are also regulated, either by the public authorities or by a central body representative of the securities industry, in such a way as to establish orders of priority for bond issues, or to ensure certain conditions under which equity issues may be made. In either case the issues of nationally-owned companies will tend to receive preference over those of foreign-controlled companies. Finally, in a number of countries, particularly in the developing areas, but also in Western Europe and elsewhere, a large proportion of the loan funds available in the bond market are furnished by state or parastatal institutions, themselves financed either from the public purse or through public savings channels. Given the provenance of these funds, loan advances go frequently in the first instance to borrowers of national origin. It is perhaps worth remarking also that the provision of loan guarantees by parents of subsidiaries lacking adequate standing in their local capital market is not an invariably attractive recourse. Such guarantees, although they may not be taken up, and thus engender an effective outflow of funds, nevertheless stand as a contingent liability on the balance sheet of the parent. This therefore constitutes a simultaneous commitment of the funds of, and an increase in the gearing of, the parent, limiting its own recourse to the capital market and providing it with no immediate financial gain. A guarantee is therefore comparable in effect to an actual loan from the parent to the subsidiary, and is not normally undertaken except in circumstances which make it unavoidable.

The conclusions to which the above observations appear to lead is that in the field of capital issues, apparent integration of the subsidiary into the national background of the country in which it is located is of doubtful practical value, since the precedence of its issues in markets regulated or financed by the authorities will be determined in relation to the true facts of its ownership. Where no controls or priorities exist, the fact or otherwise of integration will be immaterial. As regards the competitive size and standing of the subsidiary, these attributes will—questions of control and priority aside—tend to give an advantage. However, the advantage of relative prominence is best exploited in locations where private capital can be freely competed for—that is to say in the larger industrialised countries. In these countries, however, affiliates of international companies are by definition less likely to achieve prominence. In those countries where the local subsidiaries may predominate, that is to say in countries of the developing areas, capital markets in which private funds can be freely competed for are sparse or non-existent; capital funds are to a very large extent provided through state or parastatal institutions, which themselves necessarily give preference to nationally-owned enterprises.

It should perhaps be stressed that the foregoing impediments do not apply to the availability of bank credit. In this case, public controls on borrowing do not normally exist; little or no discrimination is exercised against foreign-controlled borrowers, and funds are relatively freely available in most countries. However, the present section is necessarily concerned with long-term capital.

(iii) Conclusions on Extra-Territoriality

Thus whilst long-term capital facilities remain available to international companies in the countries in which they operate, as figures furnished in preceding sections of the present study demonstrate, it appears true to say that in this field, international companies lie under handicaps which are not incurred by multi-company groups operating within the boundaries of single states. The field of capital recruitment might indeed be said to illustrate a double disability familiar to international companies: that of being regarded as nationally based for certain purposes, and, at the same time, extra-territorial for other purposes. Thus the subsidiaries of international companies remain registered, resident companies of the countries in which they are established, subject to the full range of domestic laws and regulations as regards their constitution, tax liabilities, exchange operations, method of conducting business, and so on; at the same time, their extra-territorial origin is taken into account when determining their degree of access to the capital market of the country to whose laws they are subordinated.

(c) ALTERNATIVE FINANCING

It remains to be seen to what extent international companies are able to obviate the handicaps delineated above. Clearly, there are three broad methods by which international companies might ease their own position. They may firstly reduce the overall reliance of the group on external long-term capital through an intensification of the self-financing, or cash flow, of the group; secondly, they might dilute the foreign character of the subsidiary by increasing the local ownership of its equity capital, thus at one stroke enhancing the subsidiary's ability to borrow, and reducing the parent's need to supply capital across its own country's exchange control; thirdly, the international group might look, outside domestic capital markets, to the international capital market for its funds.

(i) *Increased Self-Financing*

The highest attainable level of self-financing, or of cash flow, is the primary objective of all companies. The creation of internal resources is, as remarked upon earlier, the mechanism through which an original capital input is converted into an earnings flow, the accumulation of which, in the medium- to short-term, exceeds this initial investment outlay. The highest attainable level of self-financing, achieved through the medium of maximum dividend and other income payments from the subsidiaries to the parent, is also, as has been mentioned, the primary aim of multi-company groups. Consideration of taxation and exchange risks provide a further stimulus to international groups, as explained earlier in the present section, to direct available subsidiaries' resources into the central funds of the group. Thus on all counts so far examined, international multi-company groups will, regardless of capital recruitment questions, be intent on achieving the highest possible level of self-financing, both within the subsidiary companies themselves, and within the group as a whole. By the same token, the maximum generation of internal resources for deployment to new fixed assets, and consequently the minimum resort to external long-term borrowing, will already be the prevailing rule of action.

As a necessary corollary to the above, it is difficult to envisage how, in contemplation purely of capital market difficulties, international companies could so modify their business arrangements as to increase their level of cash flow. As was shown in Part I,[2] the cash flow of these companies compares closely with that of similarly based domestic companies, and there does not appear to be a margin of potential still to be harnessed. It should be borne in mind that once all latent cash flow has been secured through the appropriate financial procedures, then self-financing remains fundamentally as a function of the industrial and commercial activities of the firm in question. Cash flow will arise basically from the equation between turnover and operating costs; the levels of depreciation and retained earnings from which further investment can be financed will depend on the dividend needs of the company, and of course of the taxation burden imposed upon it from outside. The volume of original cash flow will therefore depend on a variety of industrial, commercial and economic factors; it will be governed by the efficiency of the company in question; by the vigour or otherwise of the industrial branch in which the company is active; and by the level of demand permitted by the public authorities in the economy as a whole. As has already been pointed out, the cash flow of individual companies will, independently of the foregoing factors, vary over the latter's own lifetime; being relatively small at the outset of the company's career, when sales turnover will still be developing; and large at a period of maturity when the company and its product are well-established: the foregoing effect will be particularly true of the element of retained earnings inside the total of cash flow. On the other side of the balance, the degree to which cash flow covers investment needs will depend on the maturity of existing fixed assets, the success of the company in marketing its product, and the prospect for extended sales in the future. Normally, needs and availability can be made to coincide in large measure. Large cash flows will, in most cases, emerge in periods of high economic demand, when future sales are reasonably assured, and further investment is indicated. However, there will be transitional periods where investment needs arise alongside low cash flows.

It will be evident from the foregoing that the predominating factor in the determination of the size of cash flow is the industrial progress of the company, and not an exogenous financial factor such as the state of external capital markets. The international company will thus exert itself, in any event, to maximise its cash flow to the limit of its capacities, and then to see whether desirable expenditure on investment leaves a margin of financing to be covered by external sources. Should such externally available resources prove to be deficient, then it is open to the company to amend its investment plans, or to take such other action as may be possible; but it will not normally be in a position so to adapt its internal structure as to change its cash flow.

[2] Page 61.

(*ii*) *Increased Minority Participation*

Shares of the Parent

Although the term does not strictly apply to both, 'minority participation' will be taken here to mean both the sale of the equity of subsidiary companies to shareholders other than the parent company, and the sale of the shares of the parent company in capital markets other than that of the latter.

The last of these two possibilities should perhaps be considered first. This would consist primarily in the sale of the parent company's shares on the capital markets of many countries, rather than predominantly—as is at present the case—on the capital market of the country of the parent company. Such sales could also be made in the international capital market proper, but this eventuality will be considered under Section (*iii*) below. The primary advantage of share issues in other countries would, of course, lie in the parent company's release from exchange control curbs placed by its own Government on the export of capital raised on the domestic market. The international diffusion of the parent company's equity will also have the advantage possibly of easing the parent company's task of capital recruitment, since a low level of Stock Exchange activity in one country might be balanced by greater demand in another. Other advantages would lie in the higher level of international participation in the ultimate control of the company, whilst still avoiding the dilution of the group management's control of its subsidiaries—studied more closely below. It should perhaps be remembered, in passing, that the international diffusion of the ownership of existing international companies is in some ways already fairly advanced. The shareholders' register of a number of large international companies already comprises participants of varying nationalities. However, the corresponding shares will have been bought, in the greatest measure, on the national Stock Exchange of the parent company through the medium of capital exported from the participant's own country. The deployment of parent's equity through the medium of local issues in separate countries might represent a more desirable method of achieving the same end.

Three major difficulties appear to lie in the way of the distribution of capital along these lines. In the first place, of course, the existence of exchange controls in the countries of issue presents a significant obstacle. International companies may indeed float new share issues on the Stock Exchanges of individual countries abroad; when, however, they come to the repatriation to the parent country of the proceeds of these issues, they will in most cases encounter exchange control bars to the removal of this capital from the country in which it is recruited. The parent company thus effectively encounters in reverse the same exchange control difficulties which led it to seek to substitute for capital-raising in its own country the recruitment of capital in other countries. Where the parent company raises its capital abroad, then the exchange controls applying there militate with equivalent efficacy against the recirculation of the capital to other parts of the group. Thus it remains broadly speaking true that unless a parent company can devote the proceeds of capital issues in a specific country abroad to its own subsidiary located in the same country, then it will not derive substantial gains from removing the locus of issue from its own country to another. Secondly, the value of the funding practicable by the parent company in any given capital market will be contingent on the size and depth of that market itself. When it is considered that as against a value of $864,000 m. and $200,000 m. for New York and London respectively, the total book value of shares outstanding on the Stock Exchanges of France, Belgium and Italy were $9,400 m., $7,200 m., and $17,400 m. respectively,[3] it might be true to say that only in the first two of the above-quoted countries can a stock market be said to exist which is sufficiently developed to provide an ample reservoir of capital funds. The third and—from the practical point of view—perhaps the main objection to the procedure, lies in the fact that dispersed recruitment of equity capital would not, except in the circumstances mentioned above, add to the total capital receipts of the parent company, since the latter would in the absence of issues on foreign stock exchanges normally raise the same amount of equity capital on its home market. The procedure outlined above would represent more a method of diffusing equity issues, than of increasing the amount of equity capital issued by the parent at any given time.

This method being excluded, for the above reasons, from the realm of practical capital-raising by the parents of international companies—at least for the time being—it remains true that the international issue of equity appears to hold out some promise for the future. The procedure, whilst to some extent facilitating the parent's equity capitalisation, would extend international ownership—thus permitting a wider international share both in the ownership and the profits of these companies. As the size and permeability of capital markets in various countries— particularly those of Western Europe—develop, so it may be expected that international companies will increasingly take advantage of the equity capital-raising opportunities so presented.

Shares of the Subsidiary

The primary consideration in this instance is group control of the subsidiary. The international company being a multi-company group, the central principle of its structure is that control—where not ownership— of the subsidiaries should be in the hands of the parent company. A situation of 100 per cent ownership of the subsidiary by the parent guaran-

[3] See *OECD Financial Statistics* No. 4, 1971.

tees absolute control. Any diminution of the parent's participation necessarily entails a potential loss of control. No clear relationship between ownership ratios and the degree of control can be established. Control of a company can be exercised where the controlling equity participant holds less than 50 per cent of the shares. A sole shareholding of, say, 30 per cent or 20 per cent can, in determined hands—and given no solidarity of views in any equal or greater shareholding percentage of the remaining capital—secure control over the company. Indeed, smaller ownership ratios than this can be postulated. On the other hand, control of a company through a shareholding as thin as that suggested above could in many instances be tenuous; a resolution of the remaining shareholding into unanimous blocks of a size larger than that of the hitherto controlling interest might occur at any time; a block of the remaining shares, sufficiently large to give control, might at any time be sold to a single bidder. Since control is of paramount importance to the parent company, it is unlikely that the latter will allow its ownership to fall below 51 per cent of the outstanding capital.

Even where control—through a sufficiently high ownership ratio—is secured, a dilution of the parent's equity share may still give rise to some adverse effects. As was mentioned above in relation to transfer pricing (page 103 Part II), minority shareholders necessarily have an interest in the income and consequent profits of the subsidiary. Where the ownership of the minority shareholding is diversified, there may be no strong pressures in favour of any given policy diverging from that thought suitable to the interests of the group as a whole. On the other hand, where the minority shareholding is concentrated in few hands, or where the subsidiary has become the subject of local attention, this pressure may be substantial. In these instances minority shareholders might call for dividend payments larger than that thought desirable by the multi-company group as a whole. To secure such higher profit distributions, minority shareholders might consequentially call for levels of prices, forms of trade, methods of production, etc., not deemed by the group to be the most suitable in the circumstances. It is of course equally possible that minority shareholders will in all cases find themselves in agreement with the overall policies pursued by the group. However, the emergence of a class of minority shareholders creates a possibility of disagreement that necessarily had not existed hitherto. For this reason again, the optimum long-term interest of the group as a whole will be best secured through the restraint of minority shareholding to the smallest equity ratio possible.

Lastly, as remarked above, the degree to which equity issues may be effected locally depends on the size and depth of the capital market; in countries whose equity securities markets may not have been very substantially developed, opportunities may be relatively restricted.

All in all, therefore, in the light of the foregoing comments, it appears that the recourse of the subsidiary company to local equity capitalisation may in practice be somewhat curtailed; and this conclusion is indeed borne out by such factual data as exists. For American companies (as shown on page 56 Part I), local equity acquisitions appear to amount to 1·5 per cent of total sources of funds in developed countries, and to about 2 per cent of such sources in developing countries. The Reddaway Report[4] suggests that total minority interests in the sample of subsidiaries taken for the study amounted on average from 1955 to 1963 to some 13 per cent. The British Department of Trade and Industry[5] shows that of the total net assets of UK-owned subsidiaries abroad, some 16 per cent was 'attributable to outside shareholders' in 1969; and that for the affiliates in the UK of foreign parent companies, the total minority ownership amounted to 10 per cent. The United States Department of Commerce[6] indicates that at end-1966, majority-owned affiliates of US companies abroad (i.e. affiliates where the US parent company had 50 per cent or more of the equity) accounted for 87 per cent of total net worth in manufacturing.

Such joint shareholdings as have arisen appear to have been dictated by a number of practical reasons. Many shared subsidiaries consist of joint ventures, i.e. companies created jointly by two parents of differing specialist abilities for the purpose of establishing a common enterprise, in which these specialities can be pooled. In other cases, a company wishing to enter a given market for the first time may ally itself with an existing company by taking a shareholding in the latter. Government policy frequently prescribes, or induces, the admission of minority interests to foreign-owned subsidiaries. Thus in certain countries, more favoured tax treatment is available for foreign-owned companies having a degree of local share participation. In other countries a given element of local share participation is formally stipulated. In certain broad areas of activity such as mining and plantations, the fact that the investment activity involves the consumption of the natural resources of the host country sometimes leads to circumstances in which an element of local equity ownership is desirable where this is not prescribed by the host government.

On the whole, it appears clear that the acceptance of minority interests has not, in the majority of companies, been actuated by a quest for additional investment capital. Both the numerical data and the range of practical motives outlined above support this conclusion.[7] The admission of min-

---

[4] *op. cit.*, page 239.
[5] *Business Monitor M4*, Overseas Transactions, 1971; Tables 35 and 39.
[6] US Direct Investment Abroad, 1966.
[7] Cf. also the Reddaway Report, page 188: 'It was almost always said by companies that minority holdings had not been used as a deliberate source of finance . . .'; Professor Lee Remmers, *op. cit.*, page 271: 'Of the many businessmen and bankers who discussed this question with us, it was rare to find one who believed that companies would choose a joint venture for financial reasons alone.'

ority equity capital does not therefore seem to provide a significant relief to the difficulties encountered by international companies in the recruitment of capital.

(iii) *International Market*

The international market comprises, in reality, a short- and medium-term credit market and a medium- and long-term capital market: the Eurodollar and Eurocurrency credit markets, and the Eurobond capital market. Since Eurocurrency credits can be rolled over a number of times, they can be used to finance short-term investment projects, or to finance the first phase of longer-term projects. The Eurobond market, consisting as it does of long-term capital available in those currencies which can be lent across frontiers without hindrance, is a ready vehicle for long-term investment projects.

The advantage of the international market lies pre-eminently in the fact that it is a source of funds free of all exchange control restrictions. The Eurodollars necessarily incur no United States exchange controls, and since they take the form of deposits held by banks in American currency, they necessarily fall outside the currency area of other countries. Other Eurocurrencies, such as Euro-sterling and Euro-francs, enjoy the same exchange control freedom, having been, as non-resident accounts, withdrawn at the outset from the currency area of their own countries. The Eurobond funds are by definition free of exchange control. Thus it is possible for a UK parent company, wishing to finance the investment project of a subsidiary in another country, to obtain funds in the currency of that country through the medium of a Eurodollar deposit. Since the UK parent's debt is denominated in dollars for repayment in dollars, no foreign exchange liability other than a contingent one falls upon the UK sterling area, and this transaction will normally be approved by UK exchange control. Similarly, no recourse is made to the capital market of the host country, since the investment is financed by the import of the funds derived from the Eurodollar transaction. Similar reasoning applies to Eurobond operations.

The international market, it will be seen from the above, lends itself particularly well to the solution of the problems attending the recruitment of capital by international companies. The difficulty inherent in the extra-territorial nature of the international companies' capital transactions—seen from the angle either of the parent company or of the subsidiary, is overcome by the simple translation of these transactions into an international arena where national considerations do not apply.

Two broad qualifications have, however, to be attached to the above conclusion. These are that firstly, the international market lends itself primarily to the satisfaction of the capital export requirements of the parent company, rather than to that of the local capital needs of the subsidiary. The international market dispenses with the exchange control barriers applied to the outward movement of capital from given currency areas. It does nothing—outside these particular transactions in themselves —to alleviate the difficulties confronting subsidiaries in the raising of capital in the markets of their host countries. It is true, in principle, that subsidiaries of international companies, unable to obtain locally the capital resources they need, may themselves become direct Eurodollar or Euro-bond borrowers. However, the size of the latter markets is such that parent companies, rather than subsidiaries, are likely to have sufficient access to funds.

Secondly, and as a corollary to the above, the international market remains small in relation either to the national markets which it supple-ments, or to the investment needs of international companies as a whole. As was shown in Part I above (pages 33–35) the total Eurocurrency market in the period 1964–68 amounted to some $3,200 m. annually. The total Eurobond market amounted to approximately $3,800 m. annually. The two markets together, therefore, offered some $7,000 m. of short- to long-term capital. As against this, the total long-term domestic capital markets of the US, UK and EEC combined, in the same period, amounted to some $45,000 m. annually.[8] Total bank credit extended in the domestic markets of the three areas averaged $39,300 m. annually.[9]

As against the $7,000 m. approximately available annually from the Eurocurrency and Eurobond markets, the financing requirements of international companies as shown in Part I above stood at some $7,000 m. annually in 1964–68 for capital exports from parents to their subsidiaries (page 21 Part I), and some $1,850 m. annually of local long- and short-term borrowing by subsidiaries in the countries where they were operating.

Thus, whether judged in relation to the equivalent facilities offered within domestic markets, or by the latent requirements of international companies, the international credit and capital markets—although they have expanded very rapidly in recent years—do not provide a particularly large reservoir of funds.

Nor should it be thought that international companies are the sole clients of the international market. Other parties, having exhausted the resources of their domestic capital market (for reasons other than those applying to international companies) or seeing other advantages in the use of the international pool of funds, have been active participants, as was shown in Part I (page 34); these have included governments, munici-palities, public utilities, nationalised industries and international organisa-

---

[8] Public and private security issues (shares, bonds and debt certificates, but excluding straight loans to companies). SOURCE: OECD, 1971.

[9] IMF International Financial Service—Country Tables, line 32c, *Claims on Private Sector* (year-to-year increase; for USA and UK 1965–69).

tions. These users accounted for over 60 per cent of total Eurobond resources. In the Eurobond market international companies borrowed $1,460 m. annually, against the annual market turnover of $3,772 m., or 39 per cent. In the Eurocurrency market international companies appear to have borrowed on average some $650 m. annually in the period 1964–68, as against the annual market turnover of some $3,200 m.—a proportion of some 20 per cent.

None the less, as the above figures imply, the international market remains as a major source of finance for international companies. This is summarised in the following table:

All International Companies

1964–68 (*Aggregate*)		$m.
Total capital transfers from parents to subsidiaries		35,000
Total international financing by parents *of which:*		10,500
Total Eurodollar borrowings by parents	3,200	
Total Eurobond issues by parents	7,300	

As will be seen, 30 per cent of all capital remitted to subsidiaries was, under this calculation, drawn by the parent companies not from their domestic capital markets, but from the international capital and credit market. Given the share of parents' capital in the total financing of the group—calculated above at some 20 per cent of the total—it follows that the share of Eurocurrency and Eurobond financing in the total sources of funds of international groups as a whole is some 5 per cent.

For the reasons earlier stated, the recourse of subsidiaries to Euro-financing, where it occurs, cannot be quantified, but if this recourse is at all substantial, then the total share of Eurofinancing in the funds of international groups as a whole will be to that extent increased. Taking the American model as an example: it follows from the figures shown above in Part I (pages 54, 55 and 62 *et seq.*) that this borrowing could be equal to the difference between total 'Funds Obtained Abroad' of $2,808 m. annual average 1964–68 (see pages 54 and 55 of Part I above), and the amount known to have been borrowed on the domestic capital markets of the countries in which the subsidiaries were operating, of $1,065 m. (Part I, page 63). This residual—$1,753 m.—would constitute a further 15 per cent of the total funding of the group in the case of American international companies. However, it is almost certain that this residual is composed, to a large extent, of trade and other credit, and that Eurofinancing will account for a very small proportion of this sum. It might on the whole be safe to assume that Eurocurrency and Eurobond financing provides some 10 per cent of the total resources of international groups.

Before leaving the subject of international financing, it is perhaps useful to review briefly the function of a new intermediary recently created by international enterprises to aid in operations in the international money and capital market. The new instrument in question is the international financial company. The need for these companies arises from the fact that the Eurobond market is still supplied in large degree by wealthy individual investors, a prime concern of whose is the avoidance of withholding taxes on the capital and interest repayable to them on their loans. In most industrialised countries such withholding taxes are applied. A number of other countries—amongst whom figure, or have figured, Luxembourg, Netherlands Antilles, and Canada—do not impose such taxes. International companies wishing to raise funds through Eurobonds have therefore frequently created companies in those countries for the sole purpose of making the issues. Their repayments of interest and capital then go to the subscribers free of tax. The immediate financial advantage goes therefore to the subscriber rather than to the international company, although the latter presumes that in so choosing the location of its issue, it will meet with better subscriptions than elsewhere.

To revert finally to the issue of parent company equity in the international market, mentioned at the beginning of the present section, a number of Eurobond issues have also been made convertible into the equity of the parent company. Although this does not introduce a new source of funds— for it is open for the investor in convertible Eurobonds to purchase the parent's equity on the latter's capital market—it does, in providing greater flexibility and lower coupons, add to the attractions of Eurobond issues.

(iv) Conclusions on the International Capital Market

The recruitment of capital appears to be an area in which international companies will remain under some disadvantage. It should not be supposed from the foregoing that international companies are compelled significantly to curtail their operations on account of these difficulties. Nevertheless, it remains apparent that their operations have to be conducted in face of difficulties which do not arise for multi-company groups operating within the boundaries of single states. The potential relief open to these companies, in the increased permeability of national capital markets, and in the development of the international money and capital markets, can be clearly discerned, but may be slow in materialising.

CONCLUSIONS

The foregoing detailed scrutiny of the financial policies and practices of international companies appears to suggest three broad conclusions:

(*a*) UNITY OF PRINCIPLE

The financing of an international company follows the broad principles common to the conduct of companies as a whole. In providing for the financial needs at various stages of a production and marketing process, the financial service of an international company performs the basic commercial functions incumbent on its counterpart in all other companies. In assembling and directing the financial resources of a number of subsidiaries, and in co-ordinating these with the finances of a parent company, and in ensuring the overall profitability of the group as a whole, the financial services of an international company follows basic principles characteristic of the multi-company group as such. The financial management of international companies takes on particular features only through the accident that its operations are conducted in areas divided by the political boundaries of national states. This brings the international company into contact with a variety of financial regimes and circumstances, major manifestations of which lie in changes of taxation liabilities, of currency employed, and in constraints upon the recruitment of capital.

(*b*) THE FINANCIAL MOTIVE

It follows from the above that companies, when extending their activities from the national to the international plane, seek advantages for themselves as producing and marketing entities, and not as financial enterprises. The producing and marketing gains no doubt arise, but financial gains are not sought, and indeed do not arise. This consequence is observable in two major forms.

Firstly, certain practices normal to the financing operations of single or multi-group companies within national boundaries become difficult, or indeed inadmissible, in the international sphere. An eminent example of this lies in the mechanism of transfer pricing, considered briefly above. This mechanism is familiar on the national plane, and has been evaluated solely in the light of its commercial efficacy or otherwise. When applied on the international plane, it has appeared in the light of a transfer of profits from one national state to another, an evasion of national taxes, or of other analogous procedures, and has been made the subject of official restraints by the fiscal, customs, and exchange control authorities concerned. Other activities, such as the striking of a profit for distribution, or the mounting of an investment project, have as shown above, when translated to the international sphere, encountered difficulties excluded from the domestic scene. Although various ways of palliating these difficulties can be found, it has emerged from the above that under the pressure of its producing and marketing objectives, the international company is required to accommodate part or all of the financial disadvantages involved.

Secondly, the international company is unable to take advantage of the opportunities for financial gain which might nominally stand open in the international sphere—such as the securing of capital gain through currency operations, and of income gain through tax evasion. In both cases the primacy of group producing and marketing needs precludes the use of these opportunities. Funds are not available for currency speculation; and marketing companies cannot alter their financing structure in order to evade tax burdens.

(c) CONFORMITY OF INTERESTS WITH GOVERNMENTS

The above would appear to suggest that international companies are wedded, ab initio, to financial needs which diverge from those of the governments of the countries in which they operate.

That this is true must remain plain. However, the truth of the proposition must be carefully defined.

Instances where the financial activities of international companies bring the latter into open and direct conflict with the national authorities of the countries involved are rare. This is because the legal authority of the appropriate government is necessarily paramount, and observed by the international companies. Secondly, it is because international companies are able, by consultation with the authorities, partially to resolve contradictions in the varied financial prescriptions to which they may become subject; and thirdly, it is because, as remarked above, the force of their industrial and commercial needs is such as impel them to accept the broad weight of those financial handicaps which arise; and finally, because in view of their industrial and commercial nature, they do not operate as pure financial enterprises, taking active advantage of opportunities for transient financial gain.

It remains none the less true that, whilst no immediate clashes arise, the best financial practice of the international companies would require circumstances different from those presented by the spectrum of national states with which they have to deal.

However, again, it might be wrong to conclude that international companies and national governments are set upon mutually divergent courses, which must lead to increasing incompatibility in the future. A useful summary of the international companies' requirements for full operational efficacy might include: the dissolution of tariffs on trade in goods and of obstacles to transfers of services between national stages; the international standardisation of company law; the harmonisation of company taxation; the integration of national fiscal systems; the co-ordination of national budgetary and cyclical policy; the institution of common monetary and commercial problems; and the creation of a single international currency. An enumeration of international companies' needs in this form might suggest exacting, if not fanciful, desires. On the other hand, this catalogue is in fact no more than a recapitulation of the main headings of the Treaty of Rome and of the various proposals, such as the Werner Plan, to which the latter has given rise. Thus the desiderata of the international companies, even when expressed in apparently extreme form, constitute no more than the political aims to which the governments, at least of Europe, have already put their signature in the interests of wider unity. In the long run, the aims of international companies and governments must necessarily be said to converge.

Statistical Appendix

TABLE 1

World Direct Investment Assets
1966

Host Country *Country of Origin*		*Developed* *Countries* *$m.*	%	*Developing* *Countries* *$m.*	%
US		36,662	60·0	18,137	63·7
UK		7,215	11·8	3,349	11·8
Others		17,239	28·2	6,981	24·5
	Total	61,116	100·0	28,467	100·0

SOURCE:
Total: OECD: DAC (68) 14. (All European countries classified as 'developed'.)
US: *Survey of Current Business,* October 1971.
UK: United Kingdom Balance of Payments 1971: Table 42 (including oil).
Others: Balance of above.

TABLE 1A

World Direct Investment Flows

Capital and Income
1964–68

OUTFLOWS		INFLOWS	
Capital			
From	$b	To	
Developed Countries	35·1	Developed Countries	26·2
Developing Countries	0·1	Developing Countries	9·5
Total	35·2	*Total*	35·7
Income			
From		To	
Developed Countries	22·9	Developed Countries	36·2
Developing Countries	13·7	Developing Countries	0·2
Total	36·6	*Total*	36·4

SOURCE: See page 14 *et seq.* of text.

TABLE 2

Direct Investment Capital Receipts
by Developing Countries
1964–68 Aggregate

	$m.
Africa	2,618
Latin America & Caribbean	4,517
Middle East	1,369
Asia and Oceania	1,679
Total	10,183

SOURCE: *Development Assistance Review*, 1971, Table VI–2 for totals 1965–68. 1964 estimated: difference between 1965–68 total as recorded in Table 2 and world total 1964–68 as recorded in Table II–2, sub-divided by region according to percentage shares 1965–68.

TABLE 3

Schedule of Direct Investment Income Earned in
Developing Countries computed on DAC Adjusted Basis

	(1) DAC (1966)	(2) IMF (1966)	(3) (1) as % of (2)	(4) IMF Total 1964–68	(5) IMF Total 1964–68 Adjusted
			$m.		
Africa	503	665·9	75·5	3,114	2,314
Middle East	580	1,476·3	39.3	7,160	2,781
Asia & Australasia	399	255·4	155·9	1,412	2,163
Latin America & Caribbean	1,430	1,700·9	84·0	8,253	6,893
Total	2,912	4,098·5	71·0	19,939	14,151

SOURCE OF DAC DATA: DAC (68) 14.

TABLE 4

Return on US Non-Petroleum Assets in Less Developed and in Developed Countries
1964-68

$m.	All Countries			Developed Countries			Less Developed Countries		
	Assets	Earnings	Yield %	Assets	Earnings	Yield %	Assets	Earnings	Yield %
1964	30,152	3,263	10·8	21,432	3,317	15·5	8,720	−54	−0·6
1965	34,176	3,630	10·6	24,592	2,555	10·4	9,584	1,075	11·2
1966	38,577	3,834	9·9	28,073	2,626	9·4	10,504	1,208	11·5
1967	42,092	3,914	9·3	30,761	2,745	8·9	11,331	1,169	10·3
1968	46,096	4,573	9·9	33,577	3,202	9·5	12,519	1,371	11·0
Annual Average	38,219	3,843	10·1	27,687	2,889	10·4	10,532	954	9·1 (Excluding 1964, 11%)

SOURCE: *Survey of Current Business*, October 1970.

TABLE 5

Reinvested Earnings
1964–68

	$m.	
	Earnings	*Reinvested*
U.S.[1]		
Developing Countries	9,709[2]	1,637[3]
Developed Countries	14,250	5,949
U.K.[4]		
Developing Countries	2,978	899
Developed Countries	4,306	2,577
Other[5]		
Developing Countries	984	197
Developed Countries	4,297	1,997
Total LDCS	13,671	2,733
DCS	22,853	10,503

[1] SOURCE: *Survey of Current Business*, October 1971, as corrected in footnotes below. Developing Countries—*Latin American Republics and Other Western Hemisphere* and *Other Areas*
Developed Countries—Remainder.

[2] *Corrected on DAC basis, viz.:*

US Oil Earnings in LDCs:	Value of Assets 1964–68 (average) $7,960 m. 10 per cent of Value $788 m.

Earnings 1964–68 = $788 × 5 = $3,940 m.

US Other Earnings in LDCs:	Total recorded oil earnings $9,271 m.

Over-recording $5,331 m.
Corrected total for total earnings in LDCS:
$15,040 − 5,331 = $9,709 m.

[3] Corrected earnings ($9,709 m.) less 'Interest, Dividends and Branch Earnings' (*Survey of Current Business*, October 1971) reduced in same proportion as earnings (i.e. by 35·5 per cent). This includes all earnings of branches both remitted and unremitted, as these are not separately distinguishable. (Probably $1,250 m. was in fact reinvested over the period.)

[4] Source DTI for reinvested earnings of subsidiaries. 'UK Balance of Payments 1971', Appendix 4, Table 50 for total reinvested earnings of subsidiaries and branches. Reinvested earnings of branches obtained by subtraction and allocated to developed and developing countries in accordance with ratio for earnings of subsidiaries. For total earnings, *Business Monitor M4*, 1971, Table 21.

Including estimate for oil earnings. Assumed pro rata to US on basis of assets held overseas (total US oil assets average 1964–68: $16,427 m.; total UK average 1963–68: $3,850 m.—SOURCE: UK Balance of Payments, 1971).

[5] Total earnings in both classes of countries ($13·7 b. and $22·9 b.; see page 154) less combined UK and US earnings. Assumed percentage reinvested same as for US/UK; i.e. developing countries 20 per cent; developed countries 46 per cent.

TABLE 6

*Direct Investment Flows in the total Balance of Payments
of the United Kingdom
1966*

		$m.
(1)	Imports of Goods and Services[6]	− 24,022
(2)	Exports of Goods and Services[6]	+ 24,255
(3)	Long-term Capital Outflow	− 1,665
(4)	Long-term Capital Inflow	+ 1,219
(5)	Total Outflows (Items 1+3)	− 25,687
(6)	Total Inflows (Items 2+4)	+ 25,474
(7)	Direct Investment Outflow[7]	− 1,041
(8)	Direct Investment Inflow[8]	+ 1,733
(9)	(7) as % of (5)	4·1
(10)	(8) as % of (6)	6·8

SOURCE: IMF.

[6] Including transfers and government transactions.
[7] Capital exports and income payments.
[8] Capital imports and income receipts.

N.B. Direct investment flows on corrected basis included throughout. Inward earnings and reinvested earnings as in Table 5. Outward earnings and reinvested earnings: non-oil earnings—IMF; non-oil reinvested earnings—HMSO UK Balance of Payments 1971; oil earnings—Rates of return as in DAC (68) 14, page 38, Table 15—Europe applied to foreign-held assets in UK; oil reinvested earnings percentage shown in Table 5. 'Total Developed Countries' applied to above earnings. Oil capital movements calculated on UK-held overseas assets and foreign-held assets in UK pro rata to US assets (less reinvested earnings).

TABLE 7

*Direct Investment Flows in the total Balance of Payments
of the European Community
1966*

		$m.
(1)	Imports of Goods and Services[9]	−65,993
(2)	Exports of Goods and Services[9]	+67,703
(3)	Long-term Capital Outflow	−2,731
(4)	Long-term Capital Inflow	+1,866
(5)	Total Outflows (Items 1+3)	−68,724
(6)	Total Inflows (Items 2+4)	+69,569
(7)	Direct Investment Outflow[10]	−1,070
(8)	Direct Investment Inflow[11]	+1,895
(9)	(7) as % of (6)	1·6
(10)	(8) as % of (5)	2·7

SOURCE: IMF.

[9] Including transfers and government transactions.
[10] Capital exports and income payments.
[11] Capital imports and income receipts.

N.B. Direct investment flows on corrected basis included throughout (but no correction for overstatement of oil earnings in developing countries, owing to absence of data on Community-held oil assets in those countries). Outward and inward direct investment reinvested earnings: outward—percentage derived from Table 5 'Other'; inward—percentage derived from Table 5 'Total—Developed Countries'.

TABLE 8

*Direct Investment Flows in the total Balance of Payments
of the United States
1966*

		$m.
(1)	Imports of Goods and Services[12]	−41,783
(2)	Exports of Goods and Services[12]	+43,514
(3)	Long-term Capital Outflow	−6,545
(4)	Long-term Capital Inflow	+1,726
(5)	Total Outflows (Items 1+3)	−48,916
(6)	Total Inflows (Items 2+4)	+45,844
(7)	Direct Investment Outflow[13]	−4,285
(8)	Direct Investment Inflow[14]	+3,389
(9)	(7) as % of (5)	8·8
(10)	(8) as % of (6)	7·4

SOURCE: IMF.

[12] Including transfers and government transactions.
[13] Capital exports and income payments.
[14] Capital imports and income receipts.

N.B. Direct investment flows, on corrected basis, included throughout. Outward earnings corrected for overstatement of oil earnings in developing countries (see Table 5, note [2]. Outward reinvested earnings calculated as in Table 5, note [3]. Inward earnings and inward reinvested earnings, *Survey of Current Business*, October 1968, page 30, Table 12. ($695 m., $339 m.)

TABLE 9

Direct Investment Flows in the total Balance of Payments of Developing Countries
1966

	(1) Imports of Goods and Services[15]	(2) Exports of Goods and Services[15]	(3) Long-Term Capital Outflow	(4) Long-Term Capital Inflow	(5) Total Outflows (Cols. 1+3)	(6) Total Inflows (Cols. 2+4)	(7) Direct Investment Outflow[16]	(8) Direct Investment Inflow	(9) (7) as % of (5)	(10) (8) as % of (6)
$m.										
Africa	−7,343	+6,950	−290	+1,068	−7,613	+8,018	−449	+578	5·9	7·2
Middle East	−6,364	+7,198	−351	+945	−6,715	+8,143	−518	+408	7·7	5·0
Asia & Australasia	−13,480	+12,441	−535	+1,813	−14,015	+14,254	−356	+344	2·5	2·4
Latin America & Caribbean	−15,361	+15,190	−836	+2,008	−16,197	+17,198	−1,277	+752	7·9	4·4
Total	−42,549	+41,768	−2,011	+5,835	−42,560	+47,603	−2,600	+2,082	6·1	4·4

SOURCE: IMF. DAC for direct investment flows.

[15] Including transfers and government transactions.

[16] Outflows = Investment income outflows on DAC adjusted basis less reinvested earnings; Inflows = Investment capital inflows on DAC adjusted basis less reinvested earnings.

N.B. Direct investment flows on DAC basis are included throughout. SOURCES: income outflow—DAC (68) 14, page 45, Table 18; reinvested earnings—percentage deriving from Table 5 applied to above; capital inflow DAC (18) 14, page 21, Table 6 (1965). There may be some slight distortion in the table in that the IMF country coverage for non-direct investment items is smaller than that of the DAC for direct investment; thus leading to larger percentages in Columns (9) and (10).

TABLE 10

Net Direct Investment Flows in Developing Countries
1964–68

$m.	Capital Receipts	Income Arisings	Rein- vested Earn- ings	True Capital Receipts	True Income Payments	Balance
Africa	+2,618	−2,314	447	+2,171	−1,867	+304
Middle East	+1,369	−2,781	537	+832	−2,244	−1,412
Asia & Australasia	+1,679	−2,163	418	+1,261	−1,745	−484
Latin America & Caribbean	+4,517	−6,893	1,331	+3,186	−5,562	−2,376
Total	+10,183	−14,151	2,730	+7,450	−11,418	−3,968

N.B. Receipts of capital and arisings of income on corrected DAC basis (see Tables 2 and 3); assuming reinvested earnings in separate regions same percentage of income arisings as for total; i.e. 19·3 per cent (see Table 5).

TABLE 11

Net Direct Investment Flows of Developed Countries
1964–68

	$b.
OUTFLOWS	
Capital Exports	
Gross	−35·1
Reinvested Earnings	+13·3
Net	−21·8
Income Payments	
Gross due	−22·9
Reinvested	+10·5
Net	−12·4
TOTAL	−34·2
INFLOWS	
Capital Imports	
Gross	+26·2
Reinvested Earnings	−10·5
Net	+15·7
Income Receipts	
Gross due	+36·2
Reinvested	−13·2
Net	+23·0
TOTAL	+38·7
NET BALANCE	+4·5

SOURCE: Page 154 and Table 5.

TABLE 12

Direct Investment Balance of the United States

	1964–68 $m.	1966 $m.
OUTFLOWS		
Capital		
Gross	24,060	5,325
Reinvested Earnings	7,586	1,449
Net	16,474	3,929
Income Payments		
Gross due	3,605	695
Reinvested	1,952	339
Net	1,653	356
TOTAL	18,127	4,285
INFLOWS		
Capital		
Gross	2,660	425
Reinvested Earnings	1,952	339
Net	708	86
Income Receipts		
Gross due	23,958	4,752
Reinvested	7,586	1,449
Net	16,373	3,303
TOTAL	17,081	3,389
BALANCE	−1,046	−896

SOURCE: *Survey of Current Business*, relevant issues.
N.B. Income receipts and reinvested earnings as in footnotes [2] and [3] to Table 5.

TABLE 13

Provisions for Depreciation and Depletion
1964–68—Annual Average

	$m. Developed Countries	Developing Countries	All Countries
United States[17]			
Mining & Smelting ⎫			
Petroleum ⎬	1,916	1,209	3,125
Manufacturing ⎭			
Other[18]	375	94	464
Total	*2,291*	*1,303*	*3,594*
United Kingdom[19]			
All industries excluding oil (Average 1966–68)	453	137	590
Oil[20]	140	191	331
Total	*593*	*328*	*921*
Other Developed Countries[21]	*929*	*586*	*1,513*
Total Depreciation	*3,813*	*2,217*	*6,028*

[17] *Survey of Current Business*, November 1970. Developed Countries: 'Canada', 'EEC' and 'Other Europe'; Developing Countries: 'Latin America and Other Western Hemisphere' and 'Other Areas'.

[18] Depreciation figures for industries other than mining, petroleum and manufacturing are not given by the Department of Commerce. However, a comparison of the total assets of the remaining industries (see Survey of Current Business, October 1970) shows that these account for 22 per cent of the total. Depreciation could therefore be estimated as a proportion of that on mining, petroleum and manufacturing (i.e. 28·2 per cent). However, since 'Other Industries' comprise financial, marketing service and transport industries, all presumably with a lower ratio of fixed to total assets than the above-mentioned industries, it has been considered wise to adopt a proportion of 15 per cent. This has been distributed between developed and developing countries in relation to the total of assets of these industries held in the respective countries. (Total assets in all countries $12·0 b; in developed countries $9·6 b; in developing countries $2·4 b. Annual average 1964–68. Percentages 100: 80: 20.)

[19] *Board of Trade Journal*, 26th January, 1968: 'Book Value of Overseas Investment' Tables 5 and 6 (Accumulated Depreciation end-1965). *Business Monitor M4*, 1971, Tables 34 and 35 (Accumulated Depreciation end-1968).

[20] Based on average overseas oil assets 1966–68. HMSO *UK Balance of Payments*, 1971, Table 42 ($4,410 m.) Depreciation assumed to be equivalent to that on US oil assets and distributed geographically in the same ratio.

[21] Depreciation assumed to equal ratio of assets Other countries/UK–US viz. total 33·5 per cent; developed countries 32·2 per cent; developing countries 35·9 per cent.

TABLE 14

Expenditure on Fixed Assets
1964–68 Annual Average

		$m.	
	Developing Countries		*Developed Countries*
US[22]	2,744		4,145
UK (excluding oil)　(336·6)		(1,195·9)	
UK (including oil)[23]	569		1,424
Other[24]	713		1,219
Total	4,026		6,788

[22] Increased by 15 per cent to cover industries other than mining, petroleum and manufacturing. (See footnote [19] to Table 13 of Statistical Appendix.)

[23] Expenditure on fixed assets assumed to be in same ratio to book values as for US.

		(1964–68 Annual Average)
		$m.
Book value of oil net assets of US	Developing Countries	7,878
	Developed Countries	8,549
Fixed asset expenditure of US oil	Developing Countries	1,181
affiliates overseas	Developed Countries	1,168
	(Average of 1964, 1965, 1967, 1968)	
Percentage fixed asset	Developing Countries	15·0%
Expenditure to book value of net assets	Developed Countries	13·6%
Book value of UK net oil assets	Developing Countries	1,546
(Total assets held in world—	Developed Countries	1,674
$3,220 m. assumed split in same		
proportion as US); annual average		
1967–68		
Thus UK fixed asset expenditure in oil	Developing Countries	232
industry	Developed Countries	228

[24] Assumed to be in same ratio to total net assets as for US and UK combined. Thus:

Totals US and UK net assets in 1966

	Developing Countries	*Developed Countries*
US (SOURCE: *Survey of Current Business*, October 1970)	18,138	36,661
UK (SOURCE: UK Balance of Payments 1971, Table 42 for total; split between developed and developing countries according to *Business Monitor M4*, Table 34, i.e. 68·3 per cent in developed countries)	5,579	12,019
Total	23,717	48,680
Total World Assets (SOURCE DAC)	28,467	61,116
Thus: percentage US/UK of total	83·3%	79·7%

Bibliography

ARNTZEN, Andreas and BUGGE, Jens, *Doing Business in Norway*, Den norske Creditbank, Oslo, 1968.

AUSTRALIAN BRITISH TRADE ASSOCIATION, THE CONFEDERATION OF BRITISH INDUSTRY, *British Investment in Australian Manufacturing Industry*, Canberra.

BANCA NAZIONALE DEL LAVORO, *Quarterly Review*, No. 88, Rome, March 1969.

BASCH, Antonín and KYBAL, Milic, *Capital Markets in Latin America: A General Survey and Six Country Studies*, Inter-American Development Bank, Praeger Publishers, New York, 1970.

BEHRMAN, Jack, N., *Some Patterns in the Rise of the Multinational Enterprise*, Research Paper No. 18, Graduate School of Business Administration, University of North Carolina at Chapel Hill, USA, March 1969.

BIRD, Richard M., *The Growth of Government Spending in Canada*, Canadian Tax Paper No. 51, Canadian Tax Foundation, 1970.

BRANSON, William H. and HILL, Jr., Raymond D., *Capital Movements in the OECD Area*, OECD Economic Outlook, Occasional Studies, OECD, December 1971.

BRASH, Donald T., *American Investment in Australian Industry*, Halstead Press Pty. Ltd., Sydney, 1966.

BROOKE, Michael Z. and REMMERS, H. Lee, *The Strategy of Multinational Enterprise*, Longman, London, 1970.

BRUNS, Dr. Georg and HUÄSER, Dr. Karl, *Internationale Währungsordnung und Kapitalmarkt*, Fritz Knapp Verlag, Frankfurt, 1972.

BUSINESS & INDUSTRY ADVISORY COMMITTEE TO OECD, *Barriers to the Issuing and Trading of Foreign Bonds and Shares on the National Capital Markets of Certain OECD Countries (and Compendium)*, BIAC, Paris, March 1969. *Second Report on the Liberalization of Capital Movements within the OECD*, BIAC, Paris, June 1970.

CUTLER, Frederick, *US Direct Investments Abroad 1966—Part 1: Balance of Payments Data*, US Department of Commerce, Office of Business Economics, Washington, D.C., 1970.

DEUTSCHE BUNDESBANK, *Monthly Report and Supplements*.

DUNNING, John H., *The Role of American Investment in the British Economy*, Political & Economic Planning, London: Broadsheet 507, February 1969. *Studies in International Investment*, George Allen & Unwin Ltd., London, 1970.

EINZIG, Paul, *The Euro-Dollar System: Practice and Theory of International Interest Rates*, Macmillan, London, 1967. *Foreign Exchange Crises: An Essay in Economic Pathology*, Macmillan, London, 1968. *Leads and Lags: The Main Cause of Devaluation*, Macmillan, London, 1968.

EUROPEAN ECONOMIC COMMUNITY, *The Instruments of Monetary Policy in the Countries of the European Economic Community*, EEC, Brussels, 1962. *La Politique du Marche Obligataire dans les Pays de la CEE: Instruments existants et leurs applications de 1966 à 1969*, Rappart d'un groupe d'experts constitué par le Comité monetaire, Bruxelles, October 1970. EEC Statistical Office, National Accounts.

GOVERNMENT OF CANADA, *The Canadian Balance of International Payments: a Compendium of Statistics from 1946 to 1965.* (Catalogue No. 67–505: Occasional), Dominion Bureau of Statistics, Ottawa, March 1967. *Foreign Direct Investment in Canada,* Government of Canada, Ottawa, 1972.

HMSO, *The British System of Taxation,* Central Office of Information Reference Pamphlet 10, HMSO, London, 1969.

INSTITUT D'ÉTUDES BANCAIRES ET FINANCIÈRES, *Institutions et Mécanismes Bancaires dans les Pays de la Communauté Économique Européenne,* Dunod, Paris, 1969.

INTERNATIONAL MONETARY FUND, *Balance of Payments Manual,* Washington, D.C., July 1961. *International Financial Statistics.*

LEVINSON, Charles, *Capital, Inflation and the Multi-nationals,* George Allen & Unwin Ltd., London, 1971.

MAY, Herbert K., *The Effects of United States and other Foreign Investment in Latin America,* An Interim Report to The Council for Latin America, Council of the Americas, New York, 1970.

MICHAEL, Walther P., *Measuring International Capital Movements,* Occasional Paper 114, National Bureau of Economic Research, New York, 1971.

MUSGRAVE, Richard A., *Fiscal Systems,* Yale University Press, New Haven, USA, and London, 1969.

NEW ZEALAND DEPARTMENT OF STATISTICS, *Monthly Abstract of Statistics.*

ORGANISATION FOR ECONOMIC CO-OPERATION & DEVELOPMENT, National Accounts of OECD Countries, 1950–68; 1953–69. OECD Development Centre: National Accounts of Less Developed Countries, 1959–68. *Problems of Measuring Private Capital Flows to Less-Developed Countries,* OECD: December 1968. *Development Assistance: Efforts and Policies of the Members of the Development Assistance Committee,* 1968, 1969, 1970 and 1971 Review. Amendments to the Code of Liberalisation of Capital Movements, OECD, June 1970. *The Capital Market, International Capital Movements, Restrictions on Capital Operations in Austria: in Denmark,* OECD Committee for Invisible Transactions, 1970.

PELLETIER, Robert, *Les Mouvements Internationaux de Capitaux a vue et a Tres Courte Terme.* Conseil Economique et Social, Paris, December 1970.

PENROSE, Edith T., *The Large International Firm in Developing Countries: The International Petroleum Industry,* George Allen & Unwin Ltd., London, 1968.

PLAZA, Galo, *Latin America in Transition: Its Relations with the Industrialized World,* The Atlantic Papers 1, The Atlantic Institute, Paris, 1971.

POLK, Judd, MEISTER, Irene W. and VEIT, Lawrence A., *U.S. Production Abroad and the Balance of Payments: A Survey of Corporate Investment Experience,* The National Industrial Conference Board, New York, 1966.

RÉAMONN, Seán, *The Philosophy of the Corporate Tax,* Institute of Public Administration, Dublin, 1970.

REDDAWAY, W. B., *Effects of U.K. Direct Investment Overseas* (Interim Report), Occasional Papers, 12, Department of Applied Economics, University of Cambridge, Cambridge University Press, 1967. *Effects of U.K. Direct Investment Overseas (Final Report),* Occasional Papers, 15, Department of Applied Economics, University of Cambridge, Cambridge University Press, 1968.

ROLFE, Sidney E., *Background Paper for the Conference on Capital Markets,* Sponsored by the Atlantic Institute and the Business Advisory Committee to the OECD, Cannes, January 1967. *The International Corporation: Rights and Responsibilities,* International Chamber of Commerce, 1969.

ROOK, A., *Transfer Pricing: A Measure of Management Performance in Multi-Divisional Companies,* Management Survey Report No. 8, British Institute of Management, London, 1971.

SAFARIAN, A. E., *Foreign Ownership of Canadian Industry,* McGraw-Hill, Toronto, 1966.

SHELL: ROYAL DUTCH/SHELL GROUP, *Some Financial Problems of the Royal Dutch/Shell Group of Companies,* Shell Briefing Service, January 1969.

SMITH, John S., *Asymmetries and Errors in Reported Balance of Payments Statistics,* International Monetary Fund, Washington, D.C., July 1967.

SOCIETY OF BUSINESS ECONOMISTS, *Internationalisation of Business*, Papers read at the Society of Business Economists' Conference at Churchill College, Cambridge, April 1971. *Society of Business Economists*, Watford, Herts., 1971.

SPITZ, Barry, *International Tax Planning*, Butterworths, London, 1972.

TUGENDHAT, Christopher, *The Multinationals*, Eyre & Spottiswoode, London, 1971.

UK CENTRAL STATISTICAL OFFICE, *National Accounts Statistics; Sources & Methods*, HMSO, London, 1968. United Kingdom Balance of Payments. Financial Statistics.

UK DEPARTMENT OF TRADE AND INDUSTRY, Trade and Industry (incorporating the Board of Trade Journal).

UNITED NATIONS, *Yearbook of National Accounts Statistics 1969*, Volume 1, *Individual Country Data*, New York, 1970.

US DEPARTMENT OF COMMERCE, *U.S. Direct Investments Abroad 1966*—Parts I and II. *Office of Business Economics*, Survey of Current Business.

WILLIAMS, R. Glynne, *Comprehensive Aspects of Taxation*, Cassell, London, 1969.

WORLD BANK, *International Development Association*, Annual Report. *International Finance Corporation*, Annual Report.

ZENOFF, David B. and ZWICK, Jack, *International Financial Management*, Prentice Hall, New Jersey, 1969.

Index